国家社科基金项目(20BYY109)和课程思政项目（B1-0224-21-001-66）资助出版

新编英美国家概况

主编　陆少兵

编者　李俊飞　成爽

WUHAN UNIVERSITY PRESS
武汉大学出版社

图书在版编目(CIP)数据

新编英美国家概况:英文/陆少兵主编.—武汉:武汉大学出版社,2023.2
(2024.1 重印)
ISBN 978-7-307-23536-6

Ⅰ.新… Ⅱ.陆… Ⅲ.①英语—阅读教学—教材 ②英国—概况
③美国—概况 Ⅳ.H319.4:K

中国版本图书馆 CIP 数据核字(2022)第 257739 号

责任编辑:谢群英 责任校对:汪欣怡 版式设计:马 佳

出版发行:**武汉大学出版社** (430072 武昌 珞珈山)
(电子邮箱:cbs22@whu.edu.cn 网址:www.wdp.com.cn)
印刷:湖北恒泰印务有限公司
开本:787×1092 1/16 印张:12.75 字数:260 千字 插页:1
版次:2023 年 2 月第 1 版 2024 年 1 月第 3 次印刷
ISBN 978-7-307-23536-6 定价:48.00 元

前　言

"英美国家概况"为英语专业必修课，主要学习英语国家地理、历史、政治、文化、经济、教育等方面的基本知识，加深对主要英语国家国情的理解，是进一步学习语言学、文学、翻译、跨文化交际等课程的基础。

英语专业学生在日常学习中会接触大量西方国家语言文化，思想不可避免地会受到西方文化影响。在培养交流能力的同时，如何实施以"课程思政"理念为指引的课程改革，培养学生科学、理性地看待西方国家社会与文化，坚定"四个自信"，成为英语课程思政的难点。

教材编写者从立德树人视角全面审视课程内容，挖掘、提炼课程内容中蕴涵的思政元素，将其与课程思政目标相结合，围绕教学重点，形成以问题为导向的专题任务，有助于发挥专业课程的隐性教育功能，实现知识传授与价值引领的有机统一。

教材围绕"一流课程"标准，提高课程挑战度，对重、难点内容设置专题，以问题为导向，有利于开展探索性、研究性学习，培养学生审辩思维能力。针对个别重点知识点和内容，突破事物、现象表层，引导学生探索、追问事物现象背后可能的原因，深入思考事物本质。

教材在编写过程中，及时收集、更新数据，紧跟英美国家最新发展动态，保障教材内容的时新性。

"英美国家概况"课程具有内容庞杂、课时有限、思政元素较多的特点。内容涉及地理、历史、政治、经济、文化等众多知识领域，对教师知识面有较高要求；学生在学习时，记忆、理解的难度较大。

基于以上特点和教学实际，本教材主要聚焦英美两国，各分为地理、历史、经济、政治、社会生活五个章节，便于教师在一学期内开展专题教学。教材内容全面、系统，同时详略得当、重点突出。社会生活章节内容较为充实，故放在最后，教师可根据课时和进程灵活选用。

由于编者水平有限，本书难免存在不足之处，敬请读者批评指正。

作　者
2022 年 10 月

1

Contents

Part One   The United Kingdom

Overview

The full and official name of the country is the United Kingdom of Great Britain and Northern Ireland, often abbreviated as U.K. Great Britain consists of England, Wales and Scotland, together with all the offshore islands. The island of Great Britain accounts for over 90% of the country's landmass.

As a nation, Britain has produced many man of letters and great literature, has given rise to the Industrial Revolution and has invented countless items of technology that have improved the quality of life. It established one of the greatest empires in history, a parliamentary democracy for others to follow. Its role and influence today has declined but English remains the world language and is widely used. It remains the world's sixth largest economy. The high quality education and creative culture attract many students and visitors from overseas each year.

National Flag of the U.K.

British National Emblem

Chapter 1   Land and Cities

> **Think and Explore**
>
> How is the climate and how does it affect the way of life there?
>
> How do major cities take shape?
>
> Take London, Liverpool or Birmingham for instance to illustrate it.

I. Location and Climate

Where is U.K. located? It is located to the northwest of European mainland, separated from the continent by the English Channel and the North Sea. It lies between 50° and 60° north latitude, and roughly between 2° east and 8° west longitude.

Surrounded by the Atlantic Ocean and the North Sea, the climate is described as a temperate and maritime one, with plentiful moisture and rainfall. As the prevailing southwesterly winds are warmed by the Gulf Stream and made moist by the Atlantic Ocean, the climate is generally mild and temperate. It is warm and damp all the year around. There is no hot summer or harsh cold winter. The summer temperature is usually around 20℃, rarely going above 32℃. The average temperature in January is around 0℃ and seldom falls below −10℃, even in northern Scotland.

Owing to the maritime climate, the weather is changeable, especially in the summer. That is why weather is a daily and safe topic to break ice among strangers and people usually take umbrellas with them in case of rain. Moreover, the mild maritime climate provides favorable conditions for grass

The English Channel 英吉利海峡

The North Sea 北海

Latitude *n.* 维度

Longitude *n.* 经度

Temperate *a.* 温和的

Maritime *a.* 海洋的

Moisture *n.* 水分

Damp *a.* 潮湿的

The Gulf Stream 墨西哥湾暖流

Break ice 陌生人之间开始交流

Tip1　描述英国气候整体特征及其对英国人生活的影响。

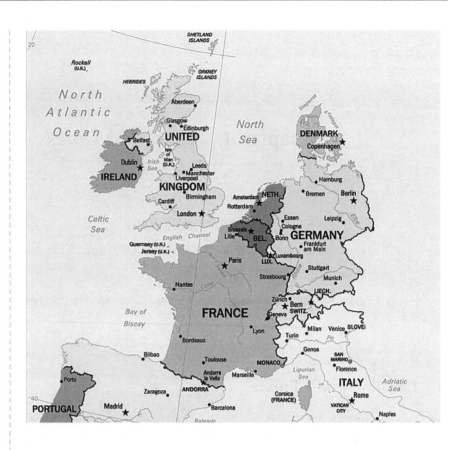

and other vegetation to grow. However, it is prone to fogs, especially in the autumn and in the winter.

There are three principal features of the climate in Britain: first, there are more rainy days but fewer sunny days; second, the fog frequently occurs in winter, for which London is famous; third is the changeability. It is difficult for people to predict what weather it will be.

II. Landscape and Water System

U.K. covers an area of about 244,100 square kilometers. It is about 966 kilometers in a straight line from the south to the north, and about 483 kilometers across the widest part. Generally speaking, the land is high in the north, the middle and the west, and low in the south and the east. The Grampians is the largest mountain range with Ben Nevis (1,344 meters), the highest mountain of U.K., situated in the Scotland. In the middle lies the

Pennines extending about 400 kilometers from the north to the south, with an average height between 200 and 500 meter above sea level, which is labeled "the backbone of England".

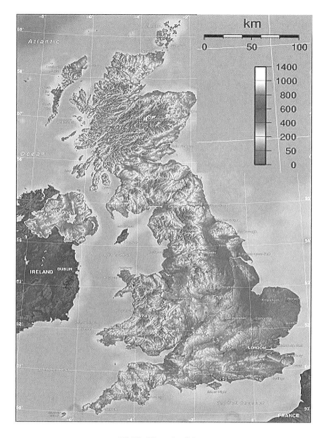

U.K. Terrain Map

When the rain falls, water will flow mostly from the north to the south, or from the west to the east. Being short and swift, few rivers in U.K. are navigable. The major rivers include the Severn in the west, the Thames in the south, and the Spey in the north.

River Thames is not the longest but the most important one. Why? River Thames(338 km), the second longest and the most important river in U.K., originates in the southwestern England and flows through the Midlands to London and empties into the North Sea. It fits large ships to travel. London is situated on the River Thames which connects the vast inner land with the sea,

Navigable *a.* 可航行的

Tip3 结合地理位置等因素,解释为何伦敦成为英国最大的城市和经济中心?

5

and allows to export goods to the European continent by ship. Thus London develops into the largest city.

Major Rivers in the U.K.

River Severn (354 km) is the longest in Britain, which starts from the mountains of Wales and runs into the Bristol Channel, where the ports of Cardiff and Bristol are located. River Mersey (110 km) flows between Lancashire and Cheshire into the Irish Sea. Its estuary, navigable for ocean vessels, is linked to Manchester by a canal with the port of Liverpool. River Clyde flows through Glasgow and River Forth passes by Edinburgh.

Glaciation *n.* 冰蚀、冰川作用

Tip4 结合英国地形地貌,理解英国交通及城市分布。

The central part of Northern Ireland is circled by highlands and mountains. On the central plains lies Lough Neagh, the largest lake of U.K. Among the highlands and mountains, due to glaciations and rainfalls, there lies many valleys and lakes. They constitute great attractions for tourists. The English Lake District is the most famous and also the largest national park in the northwest of England, close to the sea coast and the Scotland. Lake Windermere, the largest lake in England, is situated in the Lake District. William Wordsworth and other Lake Poets, enchanted and inspired by the natural scenery there, composed many classic poems.

With regard to the rugged mountain ranges, its main railways and roads are built along the eastern and western coastlines to connect the north with the south. Birmingham develops into a hub center partially because it is in the middle of the railway from London to Liverpool and Bristol. The long coastlines of Britain are dotted with many port cities like Liverpool, Edinburgh, Cardiff, Newcastle, Plymouth, Portsmouth, Newport, and Bristol.

III. Natural Resources and Cities

The main mineral resources include coal, oil, natural gas, iron ore, limestone, clay, shale, chalk and tin. Among them, oil and natural gas are the most important ones.

U.K. is one of the major producer of oil and natural gas in Europe. British Petroleum (BP) is one of the main energy dealer and provider in the world. For a long time, oil and gas were produced in the North Sea. Most of the oil produced is onshore. Long pipeline connects many oil and gas installations across the country. After a long time of drainage, the production begins to decline. U.K. has become a net importer of oil and natural gas in 2004 and 2005 respectively. Recent years, there have been discoveries and great potentials of shale, but only a few have been drilled. To solve the energy challenge, Britain is paying efforts to turn to nuclear and renewable energies.

There are various species of fish in fresh water and in the sea. Angling is a nationwide pastime in U.K., whether in lakes, on rivers or in the sea. For Britain, oceanic fishing is an important industry. Cold stream from the North Sea meets and exchanges with warm stream from the Gulf and the Atlantic, which forms the ideal place for fishes. The North Sea is an ideal and traditional fishing farm both for Britain and other European countries. However, there is dispute over the fishing right between EU members and U.K.

Tip5　思考并回答为何海洋渔业在英国经济产业中占有重要地位?

The majority of people in U.K. lives in the urban or the suburban area, distributed within the area of an ellipse extending. The top ten most populated cities are London, Birmingham, Liverpool, Nottingham, Sheffield, Bristol, Glasgow, Leicester, Edinburgh, and Leeds.

London, the capital of both England and the United Kingdom, is the political, industrial, cultural and financial center of the country. Over 8 million people live in the Greater London which composes of the City of London and 32 boroughs. The City of London, located at the center, is one of the world's leading banking and financial centers. To the east of London City is called the East End. This is an industrial area with the Port of London lying along the banks of River Thames. The West End is seated with many tourist attractions like theaters, galleries and museums, as well as business and administrative headquarters. The southern is the City of Westminster, the political center of the country. The Buckingham Palace, Westminster Abbey, Hyde Park, and Whitehall are located in the City of Westminster. Except for these, the city's landmarks include British Museum, the National Gallery, the Royal Opera House, Guildhall, St. Paul's Cathedral, Big Ben, Tower Bridge and so on.

Edinburgh is the capital of Scotland and famous for its old city partly

built in the valley of River Leith and partly on the rolling hills. Its main industries include shipbuilding, chemicals, brewing, etc. The University of Edinburgh is one of the top-rated research university in Britain.

Birmingham is the second largest city in U.K., with a population of over 1 million. It is one of the nation's leading industrial centers. Its major industries include machine tools, electrical equipment, cars and so on.

Ⅳ. Population and Languages

According to the data of population census in 2018, the total population of U.K. was about 66.5 million. The life expectancy of the British was 80 years for men and 83 for women in 2017. Compared with other countries, U.K. has one of the highest population density in the world, with about 274 persons every square kilometer, 8 times that of the United States. About 55 million people live in England, with about 9 million in London.

The majority of the population is the descendant of the Anglo-Saxons, a Germanic people who went to England between 5th and 6th centuries. The native Celtics were driven to the mountainous areas of Wales and Scotland. Some fled to the Ireland. As a legacy of British Empire, a large number of immigrants come from its former colonies in Asia, Africa and Caribbean, such as India, South Africa. In 1990s, there was a wave of immigration from Easter Europe. They have added fresh workforce. The latest immigration came from Mid East owing to the turbulence and wars. All these make U.K. an ethnically and culturally diverse country.

On the whole, English people tend to be conservative. The conservatism may be illustrated by the facts that they still keep the monarchy today and that they refuse to switch to Euro and stick to its sterling pound. People may describe them as "eccentric", "reserved", and "idiosyncratic" — all of which contain a certain amount of truth but not accurate. For the British, there continues to be a sense of pride in the glorious past and a kind of nostalgia for earlier golden times.

The major spoken languages in U.K. are English, Welsh and Gaelic.

Population census 人口普查数据

Turbulence *n.* 动荡

Nostalgia *n.* 怀旧

Tip6　如何理解英国人的"保守"?

About 20% people in Wales speaks the Welsh while some Scots and people in the Northern Ireland still speak the Gaelic. Many dialects disappeared as mass media have helped promote the use of standardized English (Received Pronunciation, or RP).

English is a member in the Germanic group of the Indo-European family. English evolved from the West Germanic group and its development can be divided into three periods: Old English, Middle English and Modern English. The Anglo-Saxons migrated to the British Isles in the 5th century. Their language is called **Old English** (450-1150), which was strongly influenced by Old Norse spoken by the Vikings and was closely related to the German and Dutch languages. It is quite different from Modern English in pronunciation, spelling and word order. The introduction of Christianity added the first wave of Latin and Greek words. The Old English period ended with the Norman Conquest when it was influenced by the French-speaking Normans.

Through the language contact after the Norman Conquest, English underwent changes: the forwarding of stress (the habit of putting stress on the root) resulted in the the loss of some inflections (grammar forms) and it borrowed many words from French and Latin. Then English entered the **Middle English** period (1150-1450). In 1204, King John lost the Province of Normandy. Norman nobles of England began to estrange from French by adopting a modified English. After the Black Death (1347-1351), the merchant and the laboring classes grew in economic and social importance, and English increased its importance compared to French. *Canterbury Tales* was written by Geoffrey Chaucer in Middle English. One interesting phenomenon was that animals began to have different names from their meat because they were raised by servants who spoke English and so kept the English names. The meat gained a French name when it was served to the French-speaking nobles and masters. For instance, "pig" became "pork", "sheep" became "mutton" and "cattle" became "beef".

As London became the center of commerce, politics and education, most books were written in London dialect and printed there. By 1450, English had entered the **Modern English** period. The printing press was introduced to England in 1476 by William Caxton, who brought standardization to English. Thanks to the printing and the first postal system established by Henry VIII in 1516, London dialect spread through the country and were accepted as the standard. Moreover, spelling and grammar were gradually fixed. The first English dictionary was published in 1604, and Samuel Johnson's dictionary — *A Dictionary of the English Language* published in 1755, was influential in establishing a standard form of spelling. English continued to assimilate foreign words throughout the Renaissance. Despite some differences in vocabulary, the written materials from the early 17th century, such as the works of William Shakespeare and *The King James Bible* are considered to be in Modern English. The Industrial Revolution and the rise of technology introduced new words in modern English for things and ideas that had not previously existed. Words like "oxygen", "protein" and "vaccine" were created using Latin and Greek roots while English roots were used for such terms as "horsepower", "airplane" and "typewriter". What's more, the rise of the British Empire and the growth of global trade gave access to words from other languages, such as "pajamas", "tycoon", "shampoo" and "sauna". The proliferation of neologism continues today, perhaps most visible in the field of electronics and computers. "Byte", "cyber-", "hard drive" and "microchip" are good examples.

Neologism *n.* 新词
Lingua Franca 通用语
Tip6　为何说英语发展史在某种程度上也是英国社会文化发展史？

Standard English is based on the speech of the southeastern England, especially the London dialect. It is also called "the Queen's English" or "BBC English" in that it is adopted as a broadcasting standard in the British media and many people regard it as a model for correct English. Standard English is codified to the extent that the grammar and the vocabulary are much the same everywhere in the world that the Singaporean, South Africa and Irish varieties differ slightly. At present, a third of the world's population use English. English has become a universal *lingua franca*.

V. Social Customs and Ethnic Diversity

Kilts *n.* 格子呢短裙
Bagpipes *n.* 风笛

Owing to the history, there exist differences among the four nations within U.K. Some Scotsmen still keep their tradition by wearing kilts and playing bagpipes. Gaelic is spoken by some people in Scotland and Northern Ireland, who regard themselves as descendants of Celts rather than Anglo-Saxons. There exist regional differences, such as the difference between the highland and lowland Scots, the northern and south England.

Christianity is the major religion in Britain. Among Christians, Anglicans are the most common denomination, followed by Catholics, Presbyterians, Methodists and Baptists. After Christianity, there are Islam, Hinduism, Sikhism, Judaism and Buddhism in terms of adherents. Most of the British social customs are based on the Christian tradition such as Christmas, Easter.

Christmas is observed on December 25th in memory of the birth of Jesus Christ. People exchange gifts with friends and relatives. Children believe that Santa Claus comes down from the North Pole to leave presents for them. Parents color boiled eggs before Easter. Later Saturday or early Sunday morning the eggs are hidden, and children will have an Easter hunt for eggs, believing the Easter rabbit comes and leaves the eggs for them.

◎ Exercises

I. Fill in the blanks.

1. The full name of the United Kingdom is the _____ and _____.

2. The island of Great Britain is made up of England, _____ and _____.

3. The United Kingdom has been a member of the _____ since 1973.

4. Britain is a society which produces a population of which 1 in 20 are of _____ ethnicity.

5. London plays a significant role in Britain's economy and culture. It's not only the financial _____ of the nation, but one of the major international financial centres in the world.

6. The capital of Britain is _____ , which has great influence on the U.K. in all fields including government, finance, and _____.

7. The capital of Scotland is _____ , which is well-known for its natural _____ .

II. Match the names of the cities in Column A with the descriptions in Column B. Put each of the letters before the descriptions in the corresponding blank in Column A.

Column A   Column B

1. (   ) Liverpool   A. the steel manufacturing center of Britain

2. (   ) Hull   B. the former center of textile industry of Britain

3. (   ) Sheffield   C. the fishing port in Humberside

4. (   ) Manchester   D. the largest city in Britain

5. (   ) Glasgow   E. the second-largest city in Britain

6. (   ) London   F. the district of Merseyside

7. (   ) Birmingham   G. the largest city in Scotland

8. (   ) Belfast   H. the capital of Wales

9. (   ) Edinburgh   I. the capital of Northern Ireland

10. (   ) Cardiff   J. the capital of Scotland

III. Give brief answers to the following questions.

1. Describe the climate in Britain and point out its major features.

2. Illustrate how the climate influences people's way of life with examples.

Chapter 2　History

Think and Explore

What is the *Magna Carta*? What's its significance?

Why is the Bourgeois Revolution also called "Glorious Revolution"?

Why did the Industrial Revolution happen first in Britain?

What can be learned from the rising and falling of the British Empire?

The British character has been shaped by its geography and two thousand years of history. Successive invasions left their mark.

I. Earliest Settlers

The earliest settlers on the British Isles were the Iberians, who came from the Iberian Peninsula between 3000 BC and 2000 BC. They left no written records and the only relic which gave evidence of their existence was the Stonehenge, built on the Salisbury Plain about 3,500 years ago.

From 700 BC, the Celts came from the upper Rhine. At least two waves of Celtic invasions can be found. First, the Gaels came over about 600 BC; second, the Britons before 300 BC. It is from the Britons that Britain gets its English name. The Celts, like the Iberians, remained tribesmen or clansmen. They knew hunting, herding, weaving, bee keeping and cultivation of wheat, oats and barley. Wars were frequent among different tribes.

Iberian Peninsula *n.* 伊比利亚半岛(今葡萄牙、西班牙所在地)

The Stonehenge *n.* 巨石阵

Tribe *n.* 部落

Stonehenge

II. Roman Britain

In 55 BC and 54 BC, Julius Caesar sent expeditions to conquer Britain for potential resources and settlement. But he did not succeed. Nearly a hundred years later, in 43 AD, the Roman Emperor Claudius succeeded and Britain became a Roman province until the beginning of the 5th century when the Roman Empire declined and finally collapsed. In 410 AD, the Roman withdrew and never returned, leaving behind some legacy: Christianity, cities and a Roman road system.

Expedition　*n.*　远 征（军）

III. Anglo-Saxon Britain and Danish Invasion

After the Roman left, Germanic tribes — the Jutes, the Angles and the Saxons landed in Britain. The indigenous Celts were pushed the mountains and England became a predominantly Anglo-Saxon society. From then on, old English spoken by the Angles and the Saxons replaced the Celtic language. The country became known as England, meaning "the land of the Angles".

The Anglo-Saxons were not Christians when they went to Britain. St.

Augustine was sent to Britain by Pope Gregory I and he arrived in Kent with 40 missionaries in 597. They completed their task and converted many Anglo-Saxons to Roman Christianity. By the late 7th century, Roman Christianity became the dominant religion in Britain.

Anglo-Saxon tribes were combined to form kingdoms. Among them, Alfred, the king of Wessex, came to gain supremacy during the process of fighting together against the Viking pirates from Denmark, Norway and Sweden — the Danish invasion. Under the leadership of King Alfred the Great, finally a peace treaty was signed in 878. Later, the balance was broken and England was ruled by Danish kings from 1017 to 1042.

Missionary *n.* 传教士
Pirate *n.* 海盗
Throne *n.* 王权
Hierarchy *n.* 等级制度
Vassal *n.* 封臣、附庸

IV. Norman Conquest

The major milestone was in 1066, when the last invasion of Britain took place. In 1066, Edward the Confessor died without an heir. His brother-in-law, Harold of Wessex, was crowned King. However, Duke William of Normandy, Edward's Norman cousin, challenged Harold's succession to the throne. William defeated the English army and killed Harold at the battle of Hastings and on Christmas Day, 1066, William was crowned King of England in Westminster Abbey, known as "William the Conquer".

The Norman Conquest marked the establishment of feudalism in England. William I adopted several measures to consolidate his ruling. After Norman Conquest, the king was the sole owner of all land, which he gave to the noble and the church in return for military and other services. The king was the lord to his vassals, who in turn were lords to his tenants. Thus a new and elaborate hierarchy of nobility was built up. He also asked not only his vassals but the vassals of his vassals to pledge loyalty to the king. What's more, he sent officials to survey each person's property and taxed according to it.

With the conquest, French became the language of the court and the ruling class and French legal, social, and institutional practice greatly influenced the English way of life. Henry II was remembered for his reform of legal system. He improved the courts of justice, introduced the jury system and institutionalized common law across the country. He also took measures to weaken the lords and knights' power. Under Henry II, the feudalism was strengthened in Britain.

V. King John and *Magna Carta*

Richard I, son of Henry II, was killed in the battle with France to regain the lost territory in 1199. His brother John succeeded the throne. In order to take revenge, King John demanded more taxes and army services. The lords were dissatisfied and forced him to sign the *Magna Carta* or the Great Charter in 1215.

The *Magna Carta* contained 63 clauses, the most important being the following 5 points: first, the King could not exact payment from the vassals without their consent; second, no freemen should be arrested, imprisoned or deprived of their freedom unless they are convicted according to the law of the land; third, merchants should be allowed to move freely; fourth, traditional rights should be given to the towns; last, if the King attempted to free himself from the law, the vassals had the right to force him to obey the law by every means possible, even by means of civil war.

Magna Carta is regarded as one of the most important sources of British constitutionalism and the spirit and some principles were still valid in U.K. nowadays. It is the first time in British history to formally limit the King's power. Though it was made to defend the interest of the privileged class, it also granted the townspeople freedom of trade and self-government.

King John's son, Henry III violated the spirit of *Magna Carta*. The outraged nobles, led by Simon de Monfort, drafted the Provisions of Oxford (later replaced by the Provisions of Westminster) and forced the King to accept it in 1258, which attempted to limit the King's power by holding regular meetings of a 15-member Privy Council. Apart from the nobles and clergymen, some common people could also join the Privy to decide on the treasury from 1264 on and later all state officials. Thus the modern idea of a

Jury *n.* 陪审团
Knight *n.* 骑士
Revenge *n.* 复仇
Magna Carta *n.* 大宪章
Convict *vt.* 定罪
Constitutionalism *n.* 宪政
Valid *a.* 有效的
The Privy Council *n.* 枢密院
Treasury *n.* 财政
Tip7　为什么说大宪章对英国具有特殊的意义和作用？

representative parliament emerged. In this sense, *Magna Carta* is regarded as the root of British politic tradition, which paved the way for its later political institutions. To some degree, the Constitutional Monarchy is related to *Magna Carta*.

VI. The Hundred Years' War and Black Death

The Hundred Years' War (1337-1453) was a series of wars fought between England and France over trade, territory, security and the throne. The English desired to regain the lost territory in France and to get a foothold in Flanders or control Flanders, an important textile market for English wool.

Charles IV, King of France, died in 1328, leaving no heir. The King of England Edward III launched the war in 1337 for the French crown under the pretext that his mother was the sister of Charles IV. At first, the war went in England's favor. When the French peasants joined under Joan of Arc, the French began to take the upper hand. By the time the war ended, the English had lost all the territories they had gained except the Port Calais.

During the long war, there were two events. One was that from 1343 on, the parliament was divided into two chambers: the House of Lords and the House of Commons. The other was that a plague, named Black Death, struck Europe and spread to England in 1348. It claimed many people's lives and resulted in the serious shortage of labour. Severe exploitation and heavy taxation led to the peasants' uprisings.

Two years after the Hundred Years' War, England was plunged into another series of civil wars, the War of Roses. It was between two great noble families: the House of Lancaster and the House of York from 1455 to 1485. Both houses fought for power, wealth, and ultimately for the throne. It lasted for 30 years. During it, open battles were few but murders and revenges were common. During the war, the common people or the economy was little affected while the old feudal nobility was greatly weakened. In the end, Henry Tudor, founder of a new monarchy, came to the throne and the House of Tudor began.

The Tudor family governed England from 1485 to 1603. Under the Tudors, England became a national state with efficient centralized government and started changing from a medieval to a modern country.

VII. The Reformation

In the 16th century, in Europe there was a movement against the Roman Catholic Church and people like Martin Luther requested a reform of the religion owing to its corruption and exploitation. The conflict was inevitable between the Rome and the King of England who established an absolute monarchy. Meanwhile there was also serious corruption in the church and the English suspected their wealth was largely taken to Rome. People's resentment of the Pope was growing. In the context, King Henry VIII brought the contradiction to the public in his appeal for a divorce. At that time, the Pope was the only person to grant the permission. However, the Pope declined. It irritated the King and started the Reformation by declaring a breakup with Rome. He suppressed the monasteries and confiscated the property of the church. In 1534 he issued *The Act of Supremacy* and declared himself the Supreme Head of the Church of England. English instead of Latin became the language for the Church. The Reformation was in essence a political movement in a religious guise.

Corruption *n.* 腐败
Divorce *n.* 离婚
Suppress *vt.* 镇压
Monastery *n.* 修道院
Confiscate *vt.* 没收
Guise *n.* 伪装
Prosecution *n.* 迫害
Appease *vt.* 缓和
Reign *n.* 统治
Tip8 英国封建社会与中国封建社会有何异同？这种差异如何影响两国的发展历程？

However, the traditional Catholicism was deeply rooted and the Reform did not go smoothly. His daughter and heir Mary I (nicknamed Bloody Mary) opposed to the reform. Bloody religious prosecution did not stop until Queen Elizabeth I, who was inclined to support Protestants, tried her best to make peace by appeasing the conflict. Under her reign, the Church of England (Anglican Church) was consolidated.

VIII. Bourgeois Revolution

British Bourgeois Revolution lasted from 1640 to 1688. During the process, many events happened, such as the two civil wars, the execution of Charles I, the establishment of the Commonwealth by Cromwell, the restoration of the Stuart and the Glorious Revolution.

1. The Background

The 15th and 16th centuries witnessed the decline of feudalism and the growth of capitalism in Britain. The Tudor Monarchy reformed the church, tolerated the Enclosure, encouraged the commerce and the exploration for colonies. Meanwhile the Renaissance was spread into England.

The Renaissance was a revival of interest in many things related to classic Greek or Roman, of which human value was stressed. It was a cultural movement led by progressive thinkers, embodying the interest of the rising bourgeoisie and working for freedom and enlightenment. One of the greatest humanists, Thomas More, wrote *Utopia* which analyzed the social contradictions in the period of capital accumulation and depicted a picture of an imaginary ideal society. Another feature with the Renaissance in Britain is that the theatre gained great popularity. William Shakespeare (1564-1616) was the greatest of the age. In his over 30 comedies, tragedies and histories, he presented with different and full views the transitional period from feudalism to capitalism.

During the period of capital accumulation, the first and most important business was the wool trade. The Enclosure Movement turned many peasants into landless men. Another way was to plunder/tap colonies. During the reign of Queen Elizabeth I, capitalism developed fast. As the bourgeoisie became powerful, they found that feudalism was hindering the further development. They wanted free trade but the monarchy controlled trade and commerce and imposed high taxes. The major clash between the parliament and the monarchy was over the monopolies that the King granted to his favorites. Things grew even worse when Charles I came to the power. In 1629, Charles I even dissolved the Parliament when the Parliament declared monopolies without its consent were illegal.

The persecution of Puritans constituted another cause. The Puritans were

The Renaissance 文艺复兴
The Enclosure Movement 圈地运动
Plunder/tap vt. 掠夺
Colony n. 殖民地
Monopoly n. 垄断

Christians who wanted to make reforms in the Anglican Church. They advocated that the common people and the King were equal before God and that free trade and individualism should be encouraged. They were persecuted and many were forced to emigrate. Some fled to America.

2. Two Civil Wars, the Restoration and the Glorious Revolution

In 1640, Charles I had to summon a parliament after 11 years to get fund to put down the rebelling Scots. Backed by the mass, the parliament refused and proceeded to struggle against absolutism. In 1642, the first civil war broke out the royalists (the Cavaliers) and the parliamentarians (the Roundheads). Oliver Cromwell led the New Model Army and defeated the King's troop. During the second civil war, Charles was recaptured and executed in 1649. The monarchy was abolished and England was declared a Commonwealth and governed as a republic.

In the period of Commonwealth, Cromwell cruelly ruled the country until he died in 1658. Seeing the uprisings which threatened the security, the bourgeoisie and the new aristocrats compromised with the rightists (Presbyterians) and invited Charles II to come back to the throne in 1660. This event is known as the Restoration of the Stuart.

When James II came to power in 1685, he tried to expand the King's power and reestablish Catholicism. These clashed with the interest of the bourgeoisie. In 1688, the two parties joined forces and staged a bloodless coup by inviting William of Orange, son-in-law of James II, from the Netherland to come and rule Britain. After William landed in England and James II fled to France, a new Parliament appointed William and Mary the joint sovereigns in 1689. This was the Glorious Revolution.

In 1689, the Parliament passed *The Bill of Rights*, which limited the power of the monarch and guaranteed the authority of the Parliament. From then on, **Constitutional Monarchy** was established and the King or the Queen ruled with power circumscribed by Parliament.

Aristocrat *n.* 贵族
Clash *v.* 冲突
Coup *n.* 政变
Circumscribe *vt.* 约束
Tip9　哪些因素导致英国资产阶级革命发生?
Tip10　英国资产阶级革命为何被称为"光荣革命"?

IX. The Industrial Revolution

Agrarian *a.* 农业的
Handicraft 手工业
Spinning Jenny 珍妮纺织机
Power loom 动力织布机
Premise *n.* 前提、条件

The Industrial Revolution refers to the process of change from an agrarian and handicraft economy to one dominated by industry and machine manufacturing. This process began in Britain in the period from 1760 to 1840 and spread to other parts of the world.

The main features were technological, socioeconomic and cultural. The technological changes included: 1) the use of new materials and energy source, chiefly coal, iron and steel, 2) inventions of new machines, such as the steam engine, spinning jenny, and the power loom that increased productivity, 3) important developments in transportation by applying steam engines, like trains, steamships.

The Industrial Revolution took root in Britain in the 18th century for a variety of reasons. After the Renaissance, people's thoughts were liberated, humanism became the prevailing thoughts which opened doors for social changes.

Britain completed the bourgeois revolution earlier, which provided the necessary political premise for the industrial revolution. After the bourgeois revolution, with the establishment of the British parliamentary system, and the promulgation of the bill of rights, the political rule of the bourgeoisie and the new aristocracy in Britain was further consolidated. Britain carried out a series of policies that were conducive to the development of capitalism, and promoted the primitive accumulation of capitalism and the arrival of the Industrial Revolution.

The Industrial Revolution is also based on the progress of natural science. From the end of the 16th century to the beginning of the 18th century, many famous scientists, mathematicians and physicists appeared in England, such as Francis Bacon and Issac Newton. Newton's three laws of mechanics solved many theoretical problems for the emergence of machines.

During the 18th century, Britain's handicraft industry has developed to a very mature stage. It not only has a large scale of production and advanced technology, but also has a meticulous division of labor and high labor productivity. This has created the necessary technical conditions for the birth of the large machinery industry.

With the advancement of natural science at that time, people's innovative consciousness gradually increased. The idea of protecting patents while people are actively investing in inventions is getting more and more attention. For example, as early as 1624, the Parliament issued a patent law to protect intellectual property rights. Because of this, more and more British people dare to invent inventions. After the discovery of the new route, European countries have organized "East India Company" to expand overseas trade and form a commercial revolution. Capitalists who pursue profits seek investment solutions for surplus funds, first in commerce, banking, shipbuilding, and then in industrial manufacturing.

Through the enclosure movement, the colonial expansion, slave trade and other means, Britain had the necessary capital, free labor force, market and other economic conditions. During this period, Britain constantly launched foreign wars, carried out slave trade and plundered wealth from the colonies. These wealth was transformed into the capital necessary for the industrial revolution.

To sum up, by the middle of the 18th century, Britain had all the necessary political, economic, scientific and technological preconditions for the industrial revolution. Therefore, the industrial revolution first took place in the U.K.

The technological and economic aspects of the Industrial Revolution brought about significant sociocultural changes. Innovations and mass production provided people with more material conveniences while enabling them to produce more, travel faster, and communicate more rapidly. It deepened the wealth gap between the rich and the poor. The employment and the subsistence became dependent on costly production means that few could afford to own. Job security was lacking: workers were frequently displaced by technological improvements and a large labour pool.

X. British Empire

The rising of the British Empire as the super global power did not happen overnight. It took a long time. Owing to the fact that Britain was an island country, Henry VIII (1509-1547) encouraged shipbuilding industry and adventurous exploration for new lands. In the Age of Exploration, he sent Cabot to explore the coast of Canada.

The Age of Exploration
大航海时代
Opportunistic *a.* 机会
主义的
Ascend *v.* 登上
The West Indies 西印
度群岛

The union of the three nations is an important part and lays the strong foundation for the rising of British Empire. In 1536-1542, during the reign of Henry VIII (his family, the Tudors, had Welsh roots), England and Wales were brought together administratively and legally. After the death of Elizabeth I in 1603, James VI of Scotland (the house of Stuart) became James I of England, uniting the two monarchies. The political union of England and Scotland took place in 1707 during the reign of Queen Anne. At that time, Great Britain took the shape we know today. In 1801, *The Act of Union* came into force, uniting Great Britain and Ireland.

The British Empire began with the colonization of Newfoundland in 1583. Early colonies were usually gained in the disguise of trade. The British East India Company is the most famous tool. Britain's great overseas trading empire dates back to the reign of Elizabeth I (1558-1603), with opportunistic acts of piracy against the rival, Spain. In 1588, the British fleet defeated the Spanish Armada. Taking advantage of the situation, the first successful English colony was established in Virginia in 1607. In the competition of expanding the colony in North America, Britain and France were involved in the Seven Years War (1756-1763). Though Britain grabbed large piece of land from France, the war was costly. To transfer the burden, Britain tried to increase the taxation on the people in the northern American colonies. It led to the American Independence War and the loss of 13 colonies. By the time Queen Victoria ascended to the throne, Britain had long been known as the First British Empire, which included the colonies in Canada, India and many small states in the West Indies.

The Victoria Age witnessed the Second British Empire. Australia, New Zealand and Canada became dominions and under the direct control of the English Crown successively in the mid 19th century. In 17th century, the East India Company seized three important Indian cities and then gradually took control of almost the whole country. From 1870s, the British government adopted an aggressive foreign policy known as the New Imperialism. In 1876, Victoria got the title of "Empress of India", leaving India her biggest and the most bright "Jewel in the Crown". India served as a gangplank for Britain to expand their colonies and sphere of influence in Asia. It was from India that the colonists shipped opium to China in exchange for tea and silk and extended their rule to Burma, Malaysia, Sri Lanka, etc. The British government launched the Opium War against China and forced the Qing government to sign the treaties, whereby Hong Kong was ceded and Britain was granted privileges for trade, travel and missionary activities in China.

In Africa, Britain took control of the Suez Canal and conquered Egypt in 1882. It also controlled South Africa where gold and diamonds had been found after the Anglo-Boer War (1899-1902). The war resulted in the creation of the Union of South Africa in 1910, the fourth self-governing dominion of the British Empire. By the end of 19th century or before World War I, the British Empire occupied about one quarter of the world's land mass and population. It also owned a large and powerful fleet, occupied the strategic spots like Gibraltar, Malta, Cyprus, Suez, Aden and reached its peak. Overseas expansion of three centuries rendered Britain the largest empire "on which the sun never set".

XI. U.K. during the Two World Wars

The world entered the period of imperialism at the beginning of 20th century. Britain's dominance was challenged by other European nations and the United States. With the development of capitalism and the imbalance of national strength among major powers, the conflict in economical and political

Dominion *n.* 领地
Gangplank *n.* 跳板
Sphere *n.* 领域、空间
Cede *vt.* 割让
Privilege *n.* 特权
The Suez Canal 苏伊士运河
The Anglo-Boer War 布尔战争
Tip12 大英帝国是如何建立的? 这一过程有何特征?
Tip13 大英帝国如何影响近代中国社会?

interests led to the two world wars in the first half of the 20th century, which greatly diminished the strength of British Empire.

Conflict of interests and colonial rivalry divided nations into two camps: **the Central Powers** — mainly Germany, Austria — Hungary, Turkey, and **the Allies** — mainly France, Britain, Russia and from 1917 the United States. World War I came to the end in 1918 but the cost was huge. A peace conference was held in Paris to discuss the arrangement after the war. To build up America's political role in the world affairs for the first time, American President Woodrow Wilson put forward a 14 points package. It turned out that his ambition and plan came across a setback. However, the League of Nations was formed to settle disputes among nations. As a part of punishment for Germany, Japan demanded colonial rights in Shandong Province, which triggered the outbreak of the demonstration on May 4th in China. Though it was in the group of the victory, Britain was drained of manpower and 70% of the merchant ships were sunk or damaged. As a result, Britain lost the sea supremacy.

World War II was a continuation of World War I. The Great Depression from 1929 to 1933 brought additional problems to Britain's economy and society. Adolph Hitler took advantage of the strong nationalism and racism in Germany and embarked on an ambitious plan to conquer Europe. Reluctant to fight another war and hostile to Soviet Union, the British government adopted the appeasement policy. The League of Nations took no substantial action to check the Fascist aggression. However, when Hitler invaded Poland in 1939, Britain and France were forced to declare war against Germany. Germany invaded France and forced it to surrender In June 1940. It turned out that the Appeasement Policy failed. At the critical moment, Winston Churchill became the Prime Minister and led the country through the hard time. Germany's attack on Soviet Union and Japan's bombing on America's Pearl Harbor propelled the two nations to join the war. With the unified efforts, **the Allies** defeated **the Axis Powers** in 1945.

Although Britain was not invaded, London and other cities were badly damaged during the air attacks. During and after the two world wars, many

Diminish *vt.* 减弱

Rivalry *n.* 竞争

Camp *n.* 阵营

Ally *n.* 盟友

Demonstration *n.* 游行示威

Be drained of 流失

Supremacy *n.* 主导地位

The Appeasement Policy 绥靖政策

Fascist *a.* 法西斯的

Invade *vt.* 入侵、侵略

Surrender *v.* 投降

Propel *vt.* 推动

Tip14 第一次世界大战发生的根本原因是什么?

Tip15 分析第一次世界大战后巴黎和会上英、美、法、日各自的意图和态度,理解山东问题为何成为五四运动的导火索。

colonies claimed their independence. For example, the independence of India and Pakistan in 1947 dismantled the Empire. Britain used to lead and dominate the world's economy since the 18th century. But its economy experienced difficulty and declined since 20th century because of the following reasons. First, Britain suffered great losses during the two world wars. It went heavily into debt to finance the wars. Second, the collapse of the British Empire sped up the decline for there was no more cheap resources or huge market any more. Third, other nations like USA rose up and stood out in the comprehensive competition. Fourth, to maintain its role and influence worldwide, Britain had to deploy military forces in many overseas locations, which was costly for a medium-sized country. Fifth, the welfare system and Labor Union somehow raised up the average costs and put Britain in disadvantageous position in the competition. Britain's strength was weakened and had to give way not only to the United States but to Japan and Germany. But the British government still wanted to maintain its past glory and to exert the influence upon the world politics. Therefore, the British Empire was replaced by the British Commonwealth of Nations, a loosely organized community of former British colonies.

Deploy *vt.* 部署
Implement *vt.* 执行
Nationalization *n.* 国有化
Inflation *n.* 通胀
Deficit *n.* 赤字
Persistent *a.* 持续的
Stagnant *a.* 停滞的
Tip16 哪些原因和事件导致了大英帝国的衰落?

XII. U.K. after World War II

In the first general election after WWII, the British people deserted the Conservative Party and Winston Churchill. In 1945, the Labor Party won the election and carried out drastic reforms and laid the foundation for the post-war British social and economic development. Economically, it implemented the nationalization of industries and exerted considerable control over private enterprises to revive the primary industries and help balance trade. However, inflation and trade deficit were persistent problems that prevented economic development, which led to the rise of unemployment. The oil crisis of 1973 brought more harms. Although the government changed from one party to another, the economy remained stagnant. In 1979, the Conservative Party under Mrs. Margret Thatcher won the general election and promised reform.

Surplus *n.* 盈余

Curb *vt.* 约束

Poll tax 人头税

Thatcher was the first woman to become Prime Minister of Britain. Her government introduced the biggest changes since WWII. She privatized state-owned industries and promoted a more competitive spirit in the British economy. Her government reduced old age pensions, shortened the period of unemployment benefits and cut child benefits. Believing that a free market and surplus labor were essentials for a successful economy, she curbed the power of trade unions. The series of policy taken by Thatcher is called **Thatcherism**.

Thatcher and her policies were, and remained, highly controversial. Her policy seemed to be a success as inflation came under control and business profits increased. 1980s saw the recovery of the British economy though it grew at lower rates than its competitors. One negative aspect of her reform was a rapid increase in unemployment. In 1982, the unemployment rate was comparable to that during the Great Depression, with 3 million people out of work. It widened the gap between the rich and the poor and increased the inequality.

As for the foreign relationships, her government took a strong stance. In 1982, in dealing with the dispute over an island, the Falklands War or Malvinas War broke out between U.K. and Argentina. Although U.K. hit hard Argentina during the war and kept the island under the reign, U.K. suffered a lot and realized that it could not afford another war. That's why it had to accept the terms over Hong Kong issue during the talk with Chinese government though Britain was unwilling and reluctant. In 1984, the *Joint Statement of the Chinese and British Governments on the Hong Kong Issue* was published. Owing to her policy and tough measures, Thatcher was also nicknamed "Iron Lady".

Thatcher served as Prime Minister until 1990 when she lost support because of the stagnant economy, the unpopular poll tax and her reluctance to integrate with the European Union. Her successor John Major followed her steps. In 1997, the Labor Party under Tony Blair went into office. Blair called for the "**Third Way**" which was different both from the old Labor Party's commitment to nationalization of economy and social welfare and from the Conservative Party's emphasis on extreme individualism. To separate politics from economic policy, Blair made the Bank of England independent. His government adopt the minimum wage and low income aids to reduce inequality. He also emphasized individual responsibility. Blair's government succeeded in limiting government expenditure, keeping inflation under control and reducing unemployment.

After World War II, Britain cooperated closely with the United States and joined the North Atlantic Treaty Organization (NATO) in 1949. As for the continental Europe, Britain adopted an isolationist policy. At first, it refused to join the European Economic Community (EEC). As Britain gradually put emphasis on trade with the European nations, in 1973 U.K. joined EEC, precursor to the European Union (EU) nowadays. However, Britain resisted European integration in 1980s and refused to adopt the single European currency, the Euro, in 1999.

Recently the U.K. has been struggling with issues revolving around multiculturalism, immigration and national identity. This is against the background of deep concerns about terrorism, religious radicalism in the late 20th century. Concerns was heightened after a series of terrorist bombings, assaults and robbery. Some advocate tough policies on limiting immigration. This diverges from the policy of EU. In 2016, U.K. votes in referendum to leave EU. This event is called **Brexit**. However, there are still many problems to solve, like the status of Northern Ireland, the issue of fishing and so on.

People in Scotland, Northern Ireland and Wales have strong sense of their nationality and demand for more recognition of their national distinctions. Scotland has always had a separate educational system, a separate legal system and the unique local administration system. The growing sense of Scottish nationalism finally led to a referendum on independence in 2014 when Britain decided to exit from European Union. Though it didn't succeed, the Scottish independence movement has continued to gain momentum since then and produced a significant impact upon British politics.

Expenditure *n.* 开支
Precursor *n.* 前身
Radicalism *n.* 极端主义
Assault *n.* 袭击
Diverge *v.* 分歧、相异
Referendum *n.* 全民公决
Momentum *n.* 动力、势头

Perplex *v.* 困惑
Grudge *n.* 积怨
Tip17 英国对欧盟采取何种态度？理解这种态度与脱欧之间的联系。

Northern Ireland is perplexed by differences between Protestants who are by far a majority and strongly attached to England and the Catholic minority who are sentimentally linked with the Republic of Ireland. After centuries of grudges and conflicts, *The Good Friday Agreement of 1998* brought hopes of lasting peace.

The death of Queen Elizabeth II in 2022, Britain's longest-reigning monarch in history, marked the end of an age. Its influence upon the future of the British Commonwealth and Scotland is in its wake.

◎ Exercises

I. Choose the best answer from the four choices marked A、B、C. and D.

1. The earliest settlers on the British Isles were the _____.

    A. Celts   B. Gaels

    C. Iberians   D. Britons

2. From 700 BC, the Celts came from the _____ and began to inhabit British Isles.

    A. Iberian Peninsula   B. Upper Rhineland

    C. Lower Rhineland   D. Scandinavian countries

3. In 43 AD, Romans under _____ conquered Britain.

    A. Julius Caesar   B. Claudius

    C. Augustine   D. the Pope

4. Roman Britain lasted until the year of _____ when all Roman troops went back to the Continent.

    A. 400 AD   B. 410 AD

    C. 445 AD   D. 449 AD

5. Which of the followings was NOT a thing of value left behind by Romans?

    A. Welsh Christianity   B. The Roman roads

    C. Cities   D. Enormous wealth

6. In the late _____ century, the Danes or Scandinavians began to attack the English coast.

    A. 6th   B. 7th

    C. 8th   D. 9th

7. The *Great Charter* was made in the interest of _____.

A. the King   B. the feudal lords

C. the townsmen   D. the merchants

8. The British Bourgeois Revolution took place in the _____ century.

A. 15th   B. 16th

C. 17th   D. 18th

9. Which of the following statements is NOT true of Puritans?

A. Puritans were Christians.

B. Puritans were opposed to Charles I and his ideas.

C. Puritans wished to purify the Church of England.

D. Puritans chose William Laud as archbishop.

10. As a result of the Industrial Revolution, which of the following statements is NOT true ?

A. Productivity was greatly increased.

B. Unskilled workers were employed.

C. Many new cities sprang up.

D. Workers' living and working conditions were improved.

11. The British Commonwealth of Nations is a / an _____ organization.

A. military   B. cultural

C. economic   D. phony

12. Which of the following terms best describes the economic situation of Britain in the 1970s?

A. Devaluation   B. Inflation

C. Stagflation   D. Debts

13. The underlying aim of Thatcherism is _____.

A. nationalization   B. denationalization

C. cutting wages   D. increasing public expenditure

II. Fill in the blanks.

1. Britain is a country with a history of invasions. In 43 AD Britain was invaded by _____ in the late 8th century they experienced raids from Scandinavia and in the 11th century they suffered invasions from _____.

2. The Anglo-Saxons began to settle in Britain in the _____ century.

3. Charles the First, King of Britain, was executed, because he attempted to overthrow _____ in the English Revolution.

4. The Glorious Revolution was actually a bloodless _____ by the bourgeoisie in the year of _____.

5. Britain's foreign policy in the years between the two World Wars was characterized by _____ the policy of _____ toward the young Soviet Union and _____ toward Fascist aggression.

6. During WWII, Britain was forced to borrow large amounts of money from _____ and _____.

7. India became independent in the year of _____.

III. Give brief answers to the following questions.

1. "British history has been a history of invasion. " How did each of the invasions influence English culture?

2. What was the British Empire? In what way is the Empire still felt in Britain and in international field?

3. What are the major causes of the decline of British economy in the 20th century?

Chapter 3　Economy

Think and Explore

What are the impacts of Thatcher's economic policy?

What's the trade relationship between the U.K. and EU members?

What are the consequences of Brexit?

Overview

The economy of the United Kingdom is a highly developed market and market-oriented economy, which has the sixth highest GDP (Gross Domestic Product) in the world. As one of the most globalized economies, its service sector is dominant which contributes 81% of the GDP. The financial service sector is particularly important, with London being the second largest financial center in the world. A total of 21 British companies are listed in the World's Top 500 Companies in 2021. There are significant regional differences in prosperity in the United Kingdom, with the South East England and North East Scotland being the wealthiest regions per capita.

The U.K. was the first country to bring about industrialization in the 18th century. It played an important role in the global economy in the 19th century through its vast colonial empire and technological superiority. The national currency of the U.K. is Pound Sterling (represented by the symbol "£", which is also known as the sterling or pound and abbreviated as GBP. The U.K. is a founding member of the G7, the G20, the International Monetary Fund, the Organization for Security and Cooperation in Europe, the World Bank, the World Trade Organization and the United Nations.

Ⅰ. Economic Policies

Strip *vt.* 除去
in disarray *n.* 混乱
Abate *v.* 减弱、减退
Tenure *n.* 任期

WWII had stripped Britain of virtually all its foreign financial resources, and the country had built up "sterling credits" — debts owed to other countries that would have to be paid in foreign currencies — amounting to several billion pounds. Moreover, the economy was in disarray. In 1945, the Labour came to power and set about some measures, such as the nationalization of railroads, docks, harbors and coal mines to promote the economy. Yet by 1947 the U.K. had been overtaken by the economic crisis, which had not abated. The loan from the United States that was supposed to last four years was nearly gone. From October 1951 to October 1964, the Conservatives remained in power for 13 years. In this period of single-party government, the themes were economic reform and the continued retreat from colonialism. After the long Conservative tenure, a Labour administration headed by Harold Wilson was established. His government inherited the problems that had accumulated during the long period of Conservative prosperity: poor labour productivity, a shaky pound, and trade union unrest. The Conservatives returned in a general election on June 18, 1970. The new prime minister, Edward Heath, set three goals: to take Britain into the European Economic Community (EEC; ultimately succeeded by the European Union), to restore economic growth, and to break the power of the trade unions. In his short term he succeeded only in negotiating Britain's entry into the EEC in 1973.

In 1979, Mrs. Thatcher was elected Prime Minister of the U.K. At the time, the U.K. was experiencing double-digit inflation, trades unions were powerful and there were signs British industry was becoming increasingly uncompetitive. In the early years of the 1980s, Mrs. Thatcher embarked on a policy of Monetarism, which involved higher interest rates and higher taxes and spending cuts. These policies were successful in reducing inflation but also led to a deep fall in output. Unemployment rose to three million and remained high throughout the 1980s, suggesting a rise in structural unemployment as a result of the decline in traditional manufacturing firms.

Mrs. Thatcher introduced economic policies that had a profound impact on the British economy. They were characterized by a belief in free-markets, an effort to reduce state intervention in the economy, reduce the power of trade unions and tackle inflation. Her main policies included the privatization of key public sector industries, deregulation of market by adopting laisse-faire, and the reduction of the power of trade unions

Privatization of key public sector industries. This includes the privatization of some of Britain's biggest companies — BP, BT, British Ga, British Airways. Shares were sold to the general public below the market price, and when the companies were floated, share-owners received an immediate increase in wealth. Critics argued the government undersold nations' resources and increase the inequality in the society.

Deregulation. Gas, electricity and telecoms were all considered natural monopolies, that is to say, the nationalized company had a legal monopoly. Deregulation meant new firms were allowed to enter the market and use the national infrastructure. Markets like telecoms became quite competitive, and real prices fell sharply. This involved opening up council services to the market. Private firms could bid for the right to run public services, so that they would have incentives to be more efficient and do the jobs at a lower cost than the inefficient public services. Critics argued private firms would cut costs to offer inferior service and make a profit at the expense of the local tax-payer.

Reduction of the power of trades unions. The coal miners' strike of 1984-1985 was a bitter battle, but Mrs. Thatcher was determined to hold out and refuse to give in to the demands of the NUM (National Union of Mineworkers). After a year-long strike, miners went back to work without receiving demands. This marked a defining moment in British industrial relations. The Thatcher government also passed legislation to make it harder to strike — policies such as banning closed shops — banning secondary picketing. It was a major victory for Thatcher and the Conservative Party, with the Thatcher government able to consolidate their economic programme.

laisse-faire policy 自由
市场经济政策
Incentive *n.* 激励
Tip18 什么是撒切
尔主义? 其影响有哪
些?

Spurious *a.* 虚假的
Unprecedented *a.* 史无前例的
Recession *n.* 经济衰退

Under Mrs. Thatcher's economic policies, inflation in the U.K. had fallen. But in order to achieve spurious money supply targets, they caused an unprecedented level of unemployment. This unemployment has caused not only personal loss but also widespread social problems. The mass unemployment, associated with inner cities, was very closely responsible for the riots which sparked across Britain in 1981.

Since 1979, the U.K. economic framework has substantially reformed in a market-friendly direction and most of the reforms were maintained after the election of the Labour government in 1997, who introduced the concept of "minimum wage" to rebalance the interests towards labors. The U.K. economy grew steadily from the early 1990s up to 2007, but then endured a deep recession during the financial crisis (2007-2008) before recovering from 2013 onwards. In 2016, British voters approved departure from the European Union by popular referendum, and the U.K. formally left the EU on January 31, 2020. *A U.K. -EU Trade and Cooperation Agreement* was concluded in December 2020, but some aspects of the future relationship remain uncertain. Services, particularly banking, insurance, and business services, are still key drivers of GDP growth. Once-large reserves of oil and natural gas are declining. Since 2017, the economic growth slowed such that the United Kingdom shifted from being one of the most rapidly growing mature Western economies to one of the slowest.

II. Agriculture

Farming is a vitally important U.K. industry making a major economic contribution, both in its own right and as a key supplier to the U.K.'s agri-food industry. In 2020, agriculture employed almost half a million people, 1.4% of the U.K. workforce and contributed £ 9.4bn (0.49%) of the total net U.K. economy, where England provided 78% of the value, Wales contributed 4%, Scotland 13% and Northern Ireland 5%. Agriculture activity occurs in most rural location, which is concentrated in the drier east (for crops) and the wetter west (for livestock). British farming is on the whole intensive and highly mechanized and 97% of farmed area is classified as conventional and 3% is classified as organic in 2020. The U.K. produces 59% of the food it consumes. The vast majority of imports and exports are made with other Western European countries.

According to the data in 2020, the utilized agriculture area was 17.3 million hectares of land, accounting 71% of the U.K. land total and about a third are arable and most of the rest is grassland. The types of farming in the U.K. can be broadly separated into three key areas:

Hectare *n.* 公顷
Arable *a.* 适于耕种的
Livestock *n.* 牲畜
Hillier *a.* 多小山的
Dairy *n.* 牛奶制品
Poultry *n.* 家禽
Rear *vt.* 喂养

- **Arable farming**. About half the arable area is cereal crops, and of the cereal crop area, more than 65% is wheat.

- **Livestock**. In 2020 63% of the total value of the U.K.'s agricultural production comes from livestock, of which dairy and beef are the largest sectors.

- **Mixed farming**. It involves a broad range of crops and livestock being grown and raised, with the advantage of fighting the risk of any one crop failing in a given year.

The varied topography and climate of England means that some sectors are more concentrated in some regions than others.

- The hillier upland regions are typically colder and wetter than the lowlands. **Sheep** are commonly farmed in hillier areas, particularly where cool summers and high rainfall are unsuitable for growing crops. 21% of England's sheepherd is in the South West and 19% in the North West.

- Moist air brings wet weather to the west of the England. The warm, wet climate and gentler hills of the west of England make it suitable for **dairy farming**. 39% of England's dairy herd is farmed in the South West.

- **Poultry** can be reared indoors and require less land compared to other types of farming. Therefore, poultry farming is less dependent on environmental factors such as climate, altitude or soil type.

- **Pig farming** is concentrated close to where the feed is produced. 37% of England's pigs are reared in Yorkshire and Humber.

- Hot air brings dry summers to the East of England. Warm summers and flat land makes the East suitable for **cropping**. 62% of England's sugar beet and 27% of wheat is grown here.

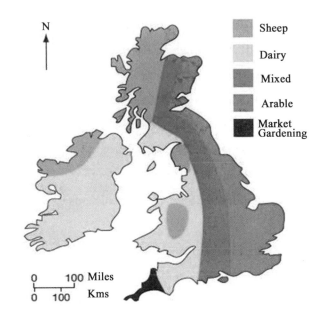

Farming Types in the U.K. (from Wikipedia)

U.K. is one of Europe's leading fishing countries but the industry has been in long-term decline. Fishing limits were extended to 200 nautical miles (370 km) offshore in the mid-1970s, and, because a significant part of the area fished by EU members lies within British waters, catches were regulated on a community-wide basis when U.K. was a EU member. At present, the fishing industry in U.K. supplies only half the country's total demand. The most important fish landed are cod, haddock, mackerel, whiting, and plaice, as well as shellfish, including *Nephrops* (Norway lobsters), lobsters, crabs, and oysters.

III. The Secondary Industries

Secondary industries are those that take the raw materials produced by the primary sector and process them into manufactured goods and products. The

British economy was primarily based on agriculture until the eighteenth century. The development of new technologies like the steam engine enabled a rapid industrialization and the growth of the secondary sector.

1. Energy Industry

In 1970s, U.K. was a net importer of energy. Following the development of oil and gas production in the North Sea, Britain became a net exporter of energy in 1981. Output fell back in the late 1980s following the Piper Alpha disaster and regained a position as a net exporter in the mid 1990s. North Sea production peaked in 1999, and the U.K. returned to being an energy importer in 2004. The contribution by the energy industries to the British economy was 2. 1% of GVA (Gross Value Added) in 2020.

In 2020, production and prices both fell due to the impact on supply and demand of the COVID-19 pandemic, however the oil and gas sector remained the second largest contributor. Of the energy total in 2020, electricity (including the renewables) accounted for 56%, oil and gas extraction 27%. In Europe, U.K. is second only to Norway in oil and gas production and over three-quarters of Britain's energy demand was met by oil and gas.

Nuclear power is expected to play an important part in helping to make sure Britain has the reliable, low carbon energy supplies it needs for the future. Currently, around 21 per cent of Britain's electricity supply is provided by nuclear power from 15 reactors. There are plans for around a quarter of Britain's energy to be supplied from nuclear plants by 2025. There is a lack of consensus in U.K. about the cost/benefit nature of nuclear energy. The long lead time between proposal and operation has put off many investments owing to its energy market regulation and nuclear waste disposal.

Reactor *n.* 反应堆
Disposal *n.* 处理、处置

BP PLC

BP PLC (formerly British Petroleum Company PLC) is a British oil and gas company headquartered in London, England. It is one of the world's seven oil and gas "supermajors". It is a vertically integrated company operating in all areas of the oil and gas industry, including exploration and extraction, refining, distribution and marketing, power generation, and trading. It operates or markets the products in more than 80 countries, .

The North Sea Oil(from *Financial Times*)

2. Manufacturing

Manufacturing is the third largest sector in its economy, after business services and the retail sector. Manufacturing industry makes up 11% of GVA (Gross Value Added), 44% of total U.K. exports, 70% of business R & D, and directly employing 2.6 million people. With an annual output of £ 183 billion, U.K. remains the 9th largest manufacturing nation in the world.

Chemicals and chemical-based products are another important contributor to U.K.'s manufacturing base. Within this sector, the pharmaceutical industry is particularly successful, with the world's second and seventh largest pharmaceutical firms (GSK and Astra Zeneca respectively) being based in the U.K. and having major research and development and manufacturing facilities there. Glaxo Smith Kline (GSK) is one of the world's largest research-based pharmaceutical corporations. The company developed the first malaria vaccine. Several products developed at GSK are in the World Health Organization's List of Essential Medicines, such as amoxicillin, mercaptopurine, pyrimethamine, and zidovudine.

Pharmaceutical *a.* 制药的

3. The Automotive Industry

The automotive industry is a vital part of Britain's economy and integral to supporting the delivery. Automotive-related manufacturing contributes £ 67 billion turnover and £ 14 billion value added to the economy, and typically invest around £ 3 billion each year in R & D. Eight out of 10 cars produced in the U.K. are exported overseas.

The U.K. is a major centre for engine manufacturing and in 2018 around 2.71 million engines were produced in the country. the U.K. has a significant presence in auto racing and motorsport industry. By the 1950s, the U.K. was the second-largest manufacturer of cars in the world (after the United States), and the largest exporter. However, in subsequent decades the industry experienced considerably lower growth than competitors such as France, Germany and Japan. Since the early 1990s, many British car marques have been acquired by foreign companies. For example, BMW acquired Mini & Rolls-Royce, SAIC MG, Tata Jaguar & Land Rover, and Volkswagen Bentley. European Union was the largest market for the U.K., both in terms of passenger cars and commercial vehicles.

4. Aerospace Industry

It is the second largest in the world and the largest in Europe. In 2020, the U.K. civil aerospace turnover totaled over $ 34.8 billion, and the sector had approximately 16% global market share. It is regarded as the crown jewel for exports and, even though the U.K. does not produce large civil aircraft, 97% of domestic aerospace production is exported.

The U.K. has a reputation as a global center of excellence for the design and production of engines, helicopters, wings, structures, and aircraft systems (including landing gear). It also designs and manufactures wings for all Airbus aircraft platforms. In addition to manufacturing, the U.K. has a thriving maintenance, repair, and overhaul sector (MRO), which provides services to the huge number of military and civil aircraft.

It is reported that over 3,000 aerospace companies operate in U.K.,

Automotive a. 汽车的
Turnover n. 营业额
Thriving a. 繁荣的
Maintenance n. 维修保养

providing over 282,000 jobs directly and indirectly. Domestic companies include BAE Systems, Cobham, GKN, Meggitt, QinetiQ, Rolls-Royce, and Ultra Electronics.

IV. Service Industry

Service industries include the retail sector, the financial sector, the public sector, business administration, leisure and cultural activities. Service industries now provide about two-thirds of the GDP and three-fourths of total employment.

1. Retailing

The U.K. is one of the leading retail markets in Europe, home to the highest proportion of international retailers and Europe's largest e-commerce market. the U.K. has the largest mobile retail sector in Europe, with 43% of retail being conducted through smart phones and tablets. The transformation of shopping has provided new opportunities in mobile retail, which is now the fastest growing segment of the retail sector in the U.K.

The U.K. has a renowned retail history and is home to everything from internationally recognized brands to artisanal small businesses. Its retail sector has proven resilient, with sales reaching £ 403 billion in 2020. London is home to prestigious shopping areas, such as Oxford Street and Mayfair, along with high-end retailers such as Tiffany & Co. and Burberry.

2. Finance

With its time zone making it easy to do business with major markets to both the east and west within the working day, the U.K. is a global centre of finance. It's the world's largest centre for international debt issuance, commercial (re)insurance and foreign exchange trading. It is also the world's leading net exporter of financial services, with 35% of financial services exports going to the EU and 31% of financial services imports coming from the EU. The sector was largest in London, where half of the sector's output was generated. A major international financial, media, and transportation hub, London is also headquarters to the European Bank for Reconstruction and Development (EBRD).

London Stock Exchange is one of the world's most international capital markets and the destination of choice for both international firms and international investors. It accounts for 43% of global foreign exchange trading and is the leading centre for international bond trading with around 79% of global secondary market turnover.

3. Trade

Trade has long been pivotal to the United Kingdom's economy. The U.K. is a member of the following international economic organizations: IMF, Commonwealth, G7, G8, G20, ICC, WHO, OECD. The total value of imports and exports represents nearly half the country's GDP (that about one-fifth of GDP of the United States). Principal British exports include machinery, automobiles and other transport equipment, electrical and electronic equipment (including computers), chemicals, and oil. Services, particularly financial services, are another major export and contribute positively to Britain's trade balance. The country imports about one-tenth of its foodstuffs and about one-third of its machinery and transport equipment.

Joining the European Economic Community caused a major reorientation of trade flows. At the beginning of the 21st century, about half of all trade was with partners in the European Union, although the United States remained the Britain's single largest export market and a major supplier (taking 20.2% of the U.K. exports). Germany was the leading supplier and the second most important export market.

In 2020, both imports and exports fell drastically (-20% and -14.6%, respectively according to IMF) owing to the outbreak of the COVID-19 pandemic, coupled with uncertainties related to the Brexit process. On May 1st, 2021, U.K.-EU trade deal came into force, granting the U.K. "zero tariff, zero quota" for its exports towards EU. Nevertheless, a series of new customs and regulatory checks have been introduced, including rules of origin and stringent local content requirements.

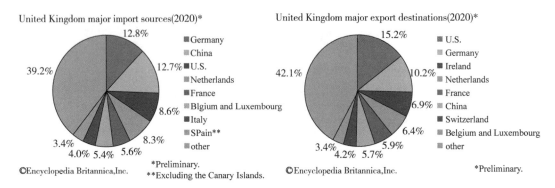

United Kingdom major import sources(2020)*
- Germany 12.8%
- China 12.7%
- U.S.
- Netherlands
- France
- Blgium and Luxembourg
- Italy
- SPain**
- other

39.2%   8.6%   8.3%   5.6%   5.4%   4.0%   3.4%

©Encyclopedia Britannica,Inc.

*Preliminary.
**Excluding the Canary Islands.

U.K.：Major Import Sources

United Kingdom major export destinations(2020)*
- U.S. 15.2%
- Germany 10.2%
- Ireland
- Netherlands
- France 6.9%
- China 6.4%
- Switzerland
- Belgium and Luxembourg
- other

42.1%   5.9%   5.7%   4.2%   3.4%

©Encyclopedia Britannica,Inc.

*Preliminary.

U.K.：Major Export Destinations

4. Consulting Industry

Management consulting is the practice of creating value for organizations by providing objective advice and implementing business solutions. It helps public and private sector organizations to become more effective and more efficient by improving how they operate, accelerating growth, reducing costs and changing the way they do their business.

Today's U.K. consulting industry is worth around £ 12.5 billion and contributes significantly to the U.K. economy. The sector is a highly skilled international workforce which is not currently replicated anywhere else in the world. The industry spans a wide array of firms, some of which only undertake "pure" management consulting work, some of which are part of larger firms that also undertake IT systems development, outsourcing, and other activities. Nowadays, the U.K. is facing a period of social, political and technological change, which means organizations have to adapt and transform more quickly than ever before.

5. Tourism

Britain's many cultural treasures—its historic castles, museums, and theatres—make it a popular tourist destination. The tourism industry is a leading sector, and each year more than 25 million tourists visit the country. London is among the world's most-visited cities and receives half of all inbound visits to the U.K. The tourism industry has been heavily affected during 2020 and 2021 by measures introduced to combat the COVID-19 pandemic.

Big Ben in London

6. Training and Education

Owing to the advantage of language and high quality education it provides, training and education has become an important revenue for the U.K. It's estimated each year over 400,000 overseas students on average come for study during the past 20 years of 21 century. Tuition, boarding fees and other expenditure bring a lot of surplus to the U.K. Moreover, the U.K. provides several global tests like IELTS and ACCA. In accordance with such tests, language and relevant training have become large and profitable business. What's more, publication and circulation of training and educational materials, such as textbooks, add more to the revenue. Training and education creates over 500,000 jobs and brings more than 250 billion pounds each year. In fact, it has become one of the pillar industries in the U.K. Owing to the promising prospect, British government has recently announced a plan to attract 600,000 international students by 2030.

◎ Exercises

I. Choose the best answer to complete each of the following statements.

1. The service industry is also called _____.

   A. subsidiary industry   B. light industry

   C. secondary industry   D. tertiary industry

2. London is the _____ financial center in the world.

   A. largest   B. second largest

   C. third largest   D. fourth largest

3. Which of the following is NOT Mrs.Thatcher's policy?

   A. Privatisation of key public sector industries

   B. Deregulation

   C. Nationalization of railroads, docks, harbors and coal mines

   D. Reduction of the power of trade unions

4. Which of the following statements is NOT true about the U.K. economy?

   A. Some smaller economies have overtaken the U.K. in terms of output per capita.

   B. Britain has experienced a relative economic decline since 1935.

   C. Britain remains one of the Group of Seven large industrial economies.

   D. There has been a period of steady decreasing of living standards.

5. Which of the following company developed the first malaria vaccine?

   A. GSK   B. BP PLC

   C. British Airway   D. BT

6. Which of the following does NOT belong to the service industry?

   A. The financial sector   B. The retail sector

   C. Business administration   D. The aerospace industry

7. Which of the following international economic organizations is the U.K. not a member of?

   A. IMF   B. SCO

   C. G7   D. OECD

8. In the aerospace industry, which of the following countries is ahead of the U.K?

A. Germany   B. France

C. The U.S.   D. Russia

9. Which of the following does NOT belong to the secondary industry?

A. The financial sector   B. Manufacturing

C. The aerospace industry   D. Energy

10. Which of the following cities is NOT an important financial center in the U.K.?

A. Glasgow   B. Oxford

C. Bristol   D. Manchester

II. Fill in the blanks.

1. _____ are commonly farmed in hillier areas, particularly where cool summers and high rainfall are unsuitable for growing crops.

2. One of the reason that makes the U.K. a global centre for finance is the _____ , which makes it easy to do business with major markets to both the east and west within the working day.

3. _____ is one of the world's most international capital markets and the destination of choice for both international firms and international investors.

4. At the beginning of the 21st century, about half of the U.K.'s trade was with the European partners, although _____ remained the United Kingdom's single largest export market.

5. In order to support the recovery of the tourism, the government has taken lot of actions to provide financial support including launching a new _____.

III. State your understandings of the following questions.

1. What are the positive and negative aspects of Ms. Thatcher's reform in the early 1980s?

2. What are the major farming types in the U.K.'s agricultural sector?

3. What are the main sectors of the U.K.'s economy?

Chapter 4   Politics

Think and Explore

What are the roles and function of the two houses?

Why is it said that the Cabinet plays the crucial role in British politics?

What are the features of British Judicial system?

I . Overview

Parliamentary
democracy 议会民
主制
Codified Constitution
成文宪法
Statutory Law 成文法
Common Law 判例法
Conventions 习惯法
Precedence *n.* 优先
地位
Clash *n.* 冲突
Deduce *vt.* 推衍、
演绎
The rule of precedent
判例拘束原则
Tip19 了解英国的
法律体系及法律构
成,理解英国法律的
特点。

Britain is a parliamentary democracy with a constitutional monarchy. Though Britain is regarded as the "Cradle of Democracy", actually it does not have a written or codified Constitution. Law in U.K. is made up of three main parts: statutory law, common law and conventions. Statutes are laws that have actually been passed by Parliament and take precedence over the others if there is a clash. Common law is deduced from customs or legal precedents and is interpreted in court cases by judges. Legal justice is largely based on what is called the rule of precedent — in order wards, what was determined in the past informs the present by way of legal ruling. Conventions are rules and practices which are not enforceable, but are regarded as vital to the working of the government. Many of the rules that govern the nation are customs or conventions. The flexibility of the British law system helps explain why it has developed so fully over the years.

October 1, 2009 marked a defining moment in the constitutional history of the U.K.: it was the date when the supreme judicial authority was

transferred away from the House of Lords and passed to a new institution —
the Supreme Court, which is the final court of appeal for civil cases and for
criminal cases in the U.K. The Supreme Court hears cases of the greatest
public or constitutional importance affecting the whole population.

The government is elected by people and governs according to British
constitutional principles and other laws. As a parliamentary democracy, the
British government is characterized by a division of powers among the
legislature, the executive and the judiciary. However, the division is not so
absolute as that in US because the Prime Minister, the head of the
government, is also the leader of the majority party in the Parliament.
Moreover, he advises the monarch on the candidates of the Supreme Court
judges.

II. The Monarch

The monarchy is the oldest institution of the British government.
Theoretically, the monarch has all the power but in reality almost all the acts
are performed on the advice of the ministers. That is to say, the King or
Queen is the head of state but the role is symbolic and ceremonial.

The importance of the monarchy rests in in its effect on public attitude. It
is regarded as a symbol of the unity of the country, an indissoluble bond
among people who retain many regional and cultural differences. It also
represents the continuity and adaptability of the whole political system. The
British are convinced that the Queen has no bias towards any nation and will
help protect people's rights, the right to private property, the right not to be
imprisoned without a trial and so on.

III. The Legislature

Parliament is the law-making body of Britain, which consists of the
Crown, the House of Lords and the House of Commons. Its main functions

Appeal *n.* 上诉
Civil case 民事案件
Criminal case 刑事案件
Hear *vt.* 审理
The legislature 立法机构
The executive 行政机构
The judiciary 司法机构
Candidate *n.* 候选人
Indissoluble *a.* 不能分解的、牢固的

are debating, making laws and supervising the government and finance. Most of the work is carried out through a system of debates, which is the same for both Houses.

The House of Lords, often referred to as the Upper House, is made up of elected hereditary peers, a limited number of 26 archbishops and bishops, and life peers. It is presided over by a Lord Speaker or Lord Chancellor. The main legislative function of the House of Lords is to examine and revise bills from the House of Commons. It functions mainly as a revising chamber.

The House of Commons, referred to as the Lower House, is the center of parliamentary power. It is composed of 650 Members of Parliament, known as "MPs" who represent 650 constituencies. The party which wins and holds the majority of seats in it will be entitled to form the government, with the party's leader as the Prime Minister. The chairperson is the also known as the Speaker. Every five years there will be general election and so is the term for the government. Whenever the government does not get the support from the Parliament for its major policy, a new election will be held and a new government will be established.

There are three major functions for the House of Commons. The most important one is drafting new laws. Although both Houses are involved in the law-making process, the House of Commons has primacy over the House of Lords, especially in the ratification of "money bills" which dictate the taxation and public expenditure. The second function is to scrutinize the actions of the government and to supervise finance. It can force a government to resign by passing a motion of no confidence. The third function is to influence future government policy.

IV. The Executive

Today, the British central government is made up of 24 departments, ministries or offices. All the ministers first of all must be MPs and then are formally appointed by the King or Queen on the advice of the Prime Minister.

Supervise *vt.* 监督

Hereditary peers 世袭贵族

Archbishop 大主教

Life peers 非世袭终身贵族

Constituency *n.* 选区

Ratification *n.* 批准

Scrutinize *vt.* 监督

A motion of no confidence 不信任动议

Tip20 英国议会上院和下院在功能上有何差异？

He is the leader of the majority party in Parliament. After each general election, the monarch will appoint the leader of the winning party as the Prime Minister and form a new government.

The Cabinet is the core of the government and British political system. It is the supreme decision-making body in the government. It decides which policies should be taken to the Parliament to become laws. After a law has been passed and ratified, the government will take the responsibility to make sure it is implemented. The Cabinet is led by the Prime Minister. All cabinet ministers are chosen by the Prime Minister from members of his party in Parliament. As the head of government, the Prime Minister controls not only the Cabinet but also Parliament in that he is the head of the majority party in Parliament and can usually influence the legislation. Since the King or Queen's power is limited and symbolic, the Prime Minister is in effect the most powerful leader in Britain.

The Cabinet meets on regular basis at 10 Downing Street, where the Prime Minister's office is located, to discuss the most important issues of the country. The Cabinet works on the principle of collective responsibility and individual ministerial responsibility. Individual ministerial responsibility means that a cabinet minister bears the ultimate responsibility for the actions of the ministry while the collective responsibility means that cabinet members must approve publicly of its collective decisions. Otherwise, he or she shall resign or be dismissed. Whenever a vote of no confidence is made in Parliament, every minister shall resign and the Cabinet will be dissolved. A new general election will be soon held. In addition to the Cabinet, the executive branch includes the Privy Council, consisting of ministers, leaders of major political parties, the Speaker, senior judges, archbishops and some important public figures. It serves as a body of advisors.

The civil service is the largest part of the executive branch. Civil service is the permanent politically neutral organization with the function to implement the ministers' decisions. It supports the government of the day regardless of which political party is in power. Civil servants are recruited through open competition. The White Hall is often referred to the Civil

The Cabinet 内阁
Resign v. 辞职
Dissolve v. 解散
Civil Service 文职部门、政府公务人员
Civil servant 公务员
Recruit vt. 招录

Service in that most departments or ministries are in or around the former Palace of Whitehall.

Unitary *a.* 单一的
Tier *n.* 层级、等级
Civil code 民法典
The accused 被告
Innocent *a.* 清白无罪的
Guilty *a.* 有罪的

The United Kingdom is a unitary state. There are two main tiers of local authority throughout England and Wales: counties and smaller districts — cities & towns. In Scotland the two-tier local government system was abolished in 1990s. Thereafter the local government has been organized through 32 unitary authorities. Northern Ireland is divided into 26 districts for local government purposes. Each of these administrated areas has its own elected council as local authority which is responsible for many public services, including local health and social services, education, town planning, consumer protection, police, the fire service, traffic management, road construction and maintenance, garbage collecting an disposal and the like. All local councils work through committees. Decisions are made by the council in general sessions. Meetings are normally open to the public.

V. The Judiciary

The Constitutional Reform Act 2005 created the Supreme Court of the Untied Kingdom and it began to work in 2009 as the highest court of appeal for all cases except that the High Court of Judiciary remains the court of last resort in Scotland for criminal cases.

There is neither civil code nor criminal code in U.K. Nowadays, most criminal laws are contained or scattered in statutes while a large part of the civil law is not. The civil law is made up of a mass of precedents and previous court decisions, interpreted in authoritative legal textbooks.

In British criminal trials, the accused is presumed innocent until proven guilty. Trials are held in open court and the accused shall be represented by a lawyer. Most cases are tried without a jury. More serious cases are tried in higher courts before a jury of 12 persons, which decides whether the accused is innocent or guilty.

Court System in England and Wales:

The Court of Appeal has two divisions: the Criminal Division and the Civil Division. The Civil Division of the Court of Appeal hears the appeals from the High Court and under certain circumstances from the County Courts. The decisions by the Court of Appeal are binding on all the other courts except the Supreme Court.

The High Court has three divisions. Queen's Bench Division handles the cases concerning contracts and torts in the region; Family Division comprises the companies court, divisional court, and the patent court; Chancery Divisions deals with the cases regarding family law, matrimony and so on. Though binding, the decisions of High Court can be appealed to the Civil Division of the Court of Appeal.

The County court handles litigations related to civil issues. The judges who presided over the cases include district or circuit judges.

Court System in Scotland:

The Court of Session is the supreme civil court ranking after the Supreme Court of the Untied Kingdom. It is also court of appeals in Scotland. The Sheriff Court is the third level civil court and sits locally.

The High Court of Judiciary is the supreme or the main criminal court and is also a court of appeal in Scotland. The Sheriff Court is the primary criminal court and sits locally. The District Court deals with cases related to minor assaults, petty theft, drunkenness, etc.

Court System in Northern Ireland:

The Supreme Court serves as the final court of appeal in both civil and criminal cases.

The Court of Appeal deals with appeals in civil cases from the High Court and with appeals in criminal cases from the Crown Court. It also hears appeals on points of law from both County Courts and Magistrates' Courts.

The High Court hear appeals in civil cases from County Courts and County Courts hear a wide range of civil actions and appeals from Magistrates' Courts. Small Claims Courts hear consumer claims and minor civil cases.

Tort *n.* 侵权行为
Chancery Division 衡平法院，大法官法院
Matrimony *n.* 婚姻
Binding *a.* 有法律约束力的
Sheriff court（苏格兰）郡法院
Magistrates' court 治安法院

Crown court 皇家刑
事法院
Preliminary *a.* 初步
的、预审的
Probation *n.* 保释
Death penalty 死刑
Dominate *vt.* 主导
Alternate *v.* 轮流
Intervention *n.* 干预
Pragmatism *n.* 实用
主义
Stance *n.* 立场、态度

The Crown Court hears all serious criminal cases while the Magistrates' Court conducts preliminary hearings in more serious criminal cases and decides on less serious ones.

If a person is found guilty of a fairly small offence, he may be placed on probation for a period — left at liberty, but under the supervision of a probation officer, who is usually a trained, professional social worker. Punishment is in the form of fines or imprisonment, and some offenders are given suspended prison sentences. The death penalty has been abolished since 1969.

VI. Political Parties

The power to run the country lies in the parliament and the cabinet, with the Primer as the most powerful leader in practice. The party whose political ideas and policies are welcomed by the majority will be elected and empowered to form the government. The Conservative Party and the Labour Party have dominated British politics and have alternated in government by playing the role of the Government and the Opposition. There are many political parties. Among them, the Conservative Party, the Labour Party and the Liberal Democrats are the main three.

Before WWII, the leadership of Britain was continually in the hand of the Conservative Party. Since then, the ruling party changed fairly frequently. Anyway, its chance of ruling the country is relatively fatter than other parties. The Conservative Party is supported mainly by those who are from upper-middle and upper class, such as landowner and big capitalists. Economically, it supports free enterprise and market. It is against too much government intervention and especially nationalization because it often leads to inefficiency. It also favors minimizing expenditures on social welfare and reducing the influence of workers' unions. Its policies are characterized by pragmatism and belief in individualism. On the general, its stance is called "right". The notable leaders include Winston Churchill in 1940s and Margaret Thatcher in 1980s.

The Labor Party was founded in 1900 and now is one of the two major political parties in U.K. It is largely supported by low and middle class, especially from workers unions. It believes in an egalitarian economy, wherein the government plays the role of a redistributive agent, transferring wealth from the rich to the poor by means of taxation and providing support for the poor. The Labor Party came into power in 1945 and had a profound effect on British society. It set up the National Health Service to provide high-quality, free health-care for all, "from cradle to grave", providing a wide range of welfare payments. Most controversially, it nationalized many industries, making a mixed economy of both private and state-owned enterprises. All these need money, so it is known as a party of high taxation. Nowadays, its policy does not tend to be so radical and comes a bit closer to that of the Conservative Party. It is known as a center-left political party. Clement Attlee and Tony Blair are famous leaders.

The Liberal Democrats was established by merging the Liberal Party and the Social Democratic Party in 1988. It can be seen as a "middle" party, occupying the ideological ground between the two major parties. Many people see it as a comparatively flexible and pragmatic choice. It stresses the need of reforming Britain's constitutional arrangements in order to build up a government more democratic and accountable.

Egalitarian *a.* 平等主义的
Re-distributive *a.* 再分配的
Controversially *adv.* 有争议地
Merger *v.* 合并
Ideological *a.* 意识形态的
Accountable *a.* 负责任的
Session *n.* 届、会议、一段时间

Ⅶ. General Election and By-election

The general election refers to the election of MPs to the House of Commons. It must be held every 5 years after the first session of the new parliament. But it is often held before that time as it is up to the parties in government when to call a general election. Reasons for calling a general election: to obtain a continuing and/or increased majority in the House of Commons for the next five years; to seek a renewal of confidence by the country in their own policies.

The whole country is divided into 650 constituencies, each of which has about 60,000 voters and only one who wins the most votes in the constituency will be elect as a MP. In each Constituency, a suitable person is appointed as Returning Officer who is responsible for compiling the registration of voters on a year basis. On election day, each voter will go to the local voting or polling station and be given the ballot to cast his or her vote, on which candidates' name are printed.

Compile *vt.* 编制
Ballot *n.* 选票
Eligible *a.* 有资格的
Campaigning activities
竞选活动
By-election *n.*补选
Vacant *a.* 空缺的

Each party usually has a local organization in the constituency. Its main job is to choose the best candidate and help him or her to win. Anyone who is eligible can join the election. It is only necessary to deposit 500 pounds, which will be lost if the candidate does not receive at least 5% of the vote. It is so designed to prevent unserious people from running for the election. Moreover, independent candidates are unlikely to stand out from the election because voters think that even if they were to win the seat, they would be powerless against the big and powerful parties in Parliament. However, in extreme cases, a vote for an independent candidate can effectively determine which party can win the majority of seats in the House of Commons and thus prevent the very party from forming the government.

When political parties launch electoral campaigns, they usually use advertisements in TV and newspapers, leaflets and door-to-door campaigning activities to promote their candidates and policies. Before the election, the main parties will also be given several 10 minutes slots to present their major polices to the public on main national televisions like BBC.

Except for the general election, a by-election occurs when a seat becomes vacant during the lifetime of a Parliament due to the resignation, expulsion, elevation to the peerage, bankruptcy, lunacy or death of the sitting Member.

◎ Exercises

I. Choose the best answer from the four choices.

1. The Conservative and the Labour parties have been in power by turns ever since _____.

    A. the end of the 19th century   B. the end of World War I

    C. the end of World War II   D. the end of the 1960s

2. Today, _____ may be seen as the party of the " middle" occupying the ideological
   ground between the two main parties.

   A. the Conservative   B. the Labour

   C. the Liberal Democrats   D. the Tory

3. The General Election in Britain is held every _____ years.

   A. 3   B. 4   C. 5   D. 6

4. Which group of people can NOT be voters in the General Election?

   A. The U.K. citizens above the age of 18

   B. The U.K. resident citizens of the Republic of Ireland

   C. Lords in the House of Lords

   D. Members in the House of Commons

5. The deposit a candidate has to pay is supposed to _____.

   A. raise money for the election

   B. prevent people from running just for a joke

   C. prevent the poor from entering Parliament

   D. encourage the rich to run

6. The party that has the majority of seats in _____ will form the Government in Britain.

   A. the House of Commons   B. the House of Lords

   C. the Privy Council   D. the Supreme Court

7. Common law in Britain may be said to consist of _____.

   A. acts passed by Parliament   B. ordinary laws

   C. previous court decisions   D. cabinet decisions

8. As a revising chamber, the House of Lords is expected to _____ the House of Commons.

   A. rival   B. complement

   C. criticize   D. inspect

9. _____ is at the center of the British political system.

   A. The Cabinet   B. The House of Lords

   C. The House of Commons   D. The Privy Council

10. Generally speaking, the British Parliament operates on _____ system.

    A. single party   B. two party

    C. three party   D. multi party

11. In Britain, the parliamentary general election is held every _____ years.

    A. three   B. four

C. five   D. six

II. Decide whether the following statements are true (T) or false (F).

1. It is no doubt that Britain is the oldest representative democracy in the world. _____

2. In Britain, the process of state-building has been one of evolution rather than revolution, in contrast to France and the US. _____

3. The oldest institution of government in Britain is the Monarchy. _____

4. The divine right of the king means the sovereign derived his authority from his subjects.

5. As the king in theory had God on his side, he should exercise absolute power. _____

6. The term "parliament" was first officially used in 1066 to describe the gathering of feudal barons and representatives from counties and towns. _____

7. Britain is both a parliamentary democracy and a constitutional monarchy. _____

8. Britain, like Israel, has a written constitution of the sort which most countries have. _____

9. Common laws are laws which have been established through common practice in the courts. _____

III. Give brief answers to the following questions.

1. What are the three functions of the House of Commons?

2. What are some of the characteristics of the British constitutional monarchy?

3. What a part does the Monarch play in the political system in the U.K.?

4. How does the Parliament exercise its power to supervise Government?

Chapter 5   Social Life

Think and Explore

What are the differences between state schools and private schools?

What are the main features of British values and attitudes?

Ⅰ. Education

Education in England remained closely linked to religious institutions until the 19th century. Nineteenth century reforms expanded education provision and introduced widespread state-funded schools. Overall responsibility for education and children's services in England rests with the Department of Education, which is accountable to Parliament. State-funded primary and secondary education are a local responsibility, generally overseen by the local authority. There is also a small private sector.

Provision *n.* 供给

Curriculum *n.* 课程规范、课程要求

1. State and Private Schools

In the U.K., state schools are funded by government and are free for all pupils while private schools charge fees to the parents of the pupils. State-funded schools follow the "National Curriculum" with main subjects including English, math and science. State schools are reviewed by the Office for Standards in Education, Child Services and Skills (Ofsted) every three years and most are organized by Local Authorities. 93% of the children in England and Wales go to "state schools". Pupils attending a state school will not have to complete an admissions examination or interview, with the exception of state grammar schools. The main types of state school include:

Grammar schools are run by the state, so are free to attend, although pupils are selected on their academic ability.

Faith schools often have a faith focus or are defined by their religious character. They follow the national curriculum, but leadership teams can create their own approach to religious studies. Staff may have to meet specific recruitment criteria, according to their faith, yet anyone can apply for a place.

Criteria *n.* 标准
Trust *n.*信托基金
Sponsor *n.* 出资人、
赞助商

Academies, run by a trust, receive funding from the government and do not charge fees. Academies can vary the national curriculum according to the needs of their learners. Academies can be supported by universities, businesses, faith groups, or voluntary groups. These sponsors work with the academy of schools to improve performance.

Alongside the state sector, a small number of private schools (often called "public schools") provide education for a small percentage of children. They have an excellent reputation for high standards of teaching and learning and almost all pupils go on to prestigious universities when they leave. Private schools are not funded by the government, and instead charge fees for attendance. By law, private schools do not have to follow the national curriculum, although many choose to do so. They may also offer boarding to students on a termly, weekly, or flexible basis. In the U.K., the most famous public schools are Eton, Harrow and Winchester.

The existence of private schools is controversial. It is argued that private schools divert gifted children and teachers and scarce financial resources from state schools and that they perpetuate economic and social divisions.

Homeschooling in the U.K.

In contrast to many European counties, homeschooling is included in the U.K. education system. Parents can homeschool their children full-time or part-time. Accordingly, a child does not need to follow the national curriculum. Still, the local council will regularly review their progress. If it is found lacking, they may serve parents with a school attendance order.

Harrow School

2. Education System

The U.K. education system is worldwide reputed for its high quality and standards. In general, the British education system has five stages of education: early years, primary years, secondary education, further education and higher education. Education is compulsory for all children between the ages of 5 and 16.

(1) Early Years Education

Since September 2010, all three and four year old children are entitled to 15 hours of free nursery education for 38 weeks in England. Early years education takes place in a variety of settings including state nursery schools, nursery classes and reception classes within primary schools, as well as settings outside the state sector such as voluntary preschools, privately run nurseries or childminders. *The Education Act* 2002 extended the National Curriculum for England to cover children's education from the age of 3 to the end of the reception year (aged 5). Early Years Foundation Stage came into force in September 2008, and is a single regulatory and quality framework for the education and care for children.

(2) Primary School Education

In the U.K., everybody aged over 5 and under 16 is obliged to attend school. This aging time frame contains two sections of the education system in the U.K.: primary and secondary school. Primary school education begins in the U.K. at age 5 and continues until age 11, some of which are split up into Infant and Junior levels. These are usually separate schools on the same site. The Infant age range is from age 5 to 7 and the Junior age range is from age 7 to 11 under the U.K. educational system.

The major goals of primary education are achieving basic literacy and numeracy among all pupils, as well as establishing foundations in science, mathematics and other subjects. Children in England and Northern Ireland are assessed at the end of the Infant level and Junior level. In Wales, all learners in their final year of Foundation Phase and Junior level must be assessed through teacher assessments.

(3) Secondary Education

Secondary education is organized in a variety of ways for children aged 11 to 19 and is free and compulsory to age 16. In most parts of U.K., secondary schools are comprehensive; that is, they are open to pupils of all abilities. After 5 years of secondary education (at about age 16), English, Northern Irish and Welsh students sit their GCSE exams (**General Certificate of Secondary Education**). Students study between 9 and 12 subjects, some of which are compulsory (English, Math, 2/3 Sciences, History/ Geography, a Modern Language, etc.). Some are chosen by students according to their abilities and preferences. The chosen subjects and the GCSE results are very important for their Further Studies (A-Level or IB) and for their university admission.

(4) Further Education

Education in the U.K. beyond the above years is called further education. Once students complete their GCSE's they have the choice to go onto further education and then potential higher education, or finish school and go into workplaces. Pupils who hope to attend universities carry on their academic study for a further two years and then sit A-levels exams (General Certificate of Education-Advanced). Most pupils try to achieve 3 to 4 A-levels in the subjects they are most proficient at. Other pupils who decide not to go to university may choose to take vocational training. The vocational equivalent of A-levels are GNVQs (General National Vocational Qualifications), which provide a preparation for work or for taking further vocational training.

(5) Higher Education

The U.K. higher education is the level of education that follows the secondary school at the hierarchy of educational system in the U.K. Around 30% of the 18 to 19 year olds enter full-time higher education. British higher education is valued all over the world for its renowned standards and quality. Some universities are ranked at the top in the world. With its four universities being ranked in the world's top ten, London has the highest number of top worldwide ranked universities per city.

There is a difference between college and university. Here, a college is a further education institution which prepares its students to earn degrees, while a university is licensed for students to gain a degree. Universities historically have been independent and self-governing; however, they have close links with the government because a large proportion of their income derives from public funds.

Public funds flow to universities through recurrent grants and in the form of tuition fees; universities also derive income from foreign students and from various private-sector sources. After a major expansion in the 1960s, the system came under pressure in the 1980s. Public funding became more restricted, and the grant system no longer supported students adequately.

Open University is a degree-granting institution that provides courses of study for adults through television, radio, and local study programs. Applicants must apply for a number of places limited at any time by the availability of teachers.

In the U.K., a bachelors degree normally takes three years to complete and most are awarded at honour level. State colleges offer some 2-year vocational diplomas that grant exemption from the first and sometimes second year of a degree programme. Postgraduate courses in the U.K. education

Equivalent *a.* 相等的
Tuition fees 学费
Applicant *n.* 申请者
Bachelor *n.* 学士
Diploma *n.* 文凭
Degree *n.* 学位
Exemption *n.* 免除

system are very intensive. This means that the courses are usually much shorter than in other countries. A master's degree typically takes 12 months to complete. An MBA (Master of Business Administration) is a high profile course which can take 2 years. Applicants will usually be high achieving with at least 2 years managerial experience. A PhD research degree in the U.K. can take between 2 and 7 years.

Cambridge University

II. Media

For most British people, a day begins with the morning newspaper and ends with television. It is obvious that the media is central to British leisure culture. U.K. possesses one of the most universally respected and widely read national presses. In addition, the British press remains one of the freest and most diverse in the world.

1. Newspapers

The history of British newspapers dates to the 17th century with the *emergence of regular publications covering news and gossip.* The relaxation of government censorship in the late 17th century led to a rise in publications. *The Times* began publication in 1785 and became the leading newspaper of the early 19th century, before the lifting of taxes on newspapers and technological innovations led to a boom in newspaper publishing in the late 19th century. Mass education and increasing affluence led to new papers such as the *Daily Mail* emerging at the end of the 19th century, aimed at lower middle-class readers.

In the 1980s national newspapers began to move out of Fleet Street, the traditional home of the British national press since the 18th century. By the early 21st century newspaper circulation began to decline. In the early 2010s many British newspapers were implicated in a major phone hacking scandal which led to the closure of the *News of the World* after 168 years of publication and the *Leveson Inquiry* into press standards.

Broadsheet and Tabloid Newspapers

Broadsheet newspapers are broadly defined as those who write in depth for an audience interested in serious news writing rather than celebrity gossip or sensationalism. Traditionally, they were published in on a large "broad sheet". The newspapers in this category are *The Guardian*, *The Telegraph*, *The Times*, *The Financial Times* and *The Independent*.

The Guardian is the newspaper most associated with liberal middle-class Britain. Their investigative journalism is some of the best in the business, and the newspaper won with Pulitzer Prize for public-service reporting in 2014. Their popular style guide is written with a sense of humour.

The Telegraph is a right-wing paper. It has been accused of playing too much to the desires of its advertisers (including not printing important stories about criticisms of their business practices), but its reporting is otherwise well-regarded.

The Times is one of the oldest newspapers in Britain. If you want to know what contemporary opinion was of any time in the past 200 years of British history, *The Times* is a good place to start.

Emergence *n.* 出现
Cover *vt.* 报道
Gossip *n.* 流言
Censorship *n.* 审查（机制）
Boom *n.* 激增、繁荣
Affluence *n.* 富足
Circulation *n.* 发行量
Phone hacking scandal 电话窃听门事件
Tabloid *n.* 通俗小报
Celebrity *n.* 名人
Sensationalism *n.* 追求轰动效应

The Financial Times. As the name would suggest, business and economic news are its priority. It's known for the distinctive pink paper on which it is printed.

All **tabloid newspapers** are published in tabloid format. These are cheaper newspapers and quicker to read, with the balance of news versus other content (gossip, weather, sport and games such as crosswords and sudoku) tipped much more towards the latter in comparison with broadsheets.

The Daily Mail. Its website, Mail Online, is the most visited English-language newspaper website in the world. Its "Sidebar of Shame" — a section of the website that focuses mostly on the failings of celebrities — is one of the key draws for its 11 million daily visitors.

The Express. At the moment, it's notable as the most Eurosceptic newspaper in Britain, with 66% of its readers backing Brexit (the opposite end of the scale to *The Guardian*, with 75% of its readers backing Remain).

The Mirror. It's currently Britain's most popular left-wing tabloid by quite some margin. It was initially launched as a newspaper by women, for women, but this was not a commercial success, so it moved to a broader focus not long after its launch. Though the Mirror is no more reliable than its other tabloid rivals, it tends to escape the harshness of criticism targeted at *The Daily Mail* and *The Express*, possibly because of its relatively lonely political position among the tabloid market.

The Sun. Having been founded in 1964, it is relatively new. As Britain's most-read newspaper, it is owned by the same group as *The Times*. *The Sun* is the paper to keep an eye on if you want to know the mainstream of British public opinion. The paper claims that its record of endorsing election winners is because of its influence (take its famous 1992 headline on the surprise election of John Major — "It's the Sun Wot Won It").

2. TVs

The first British television broadcast was made by Baird Television's electro-mechanical system over the BBC radio transmitter in September 1929. On August 22, 1932, the BBC launched its own regular service using Baird's

30-line electro-mechanical system, continuing until September 11, 1935. The outbreak of the Second World War caused the BBC service to be suspended on September 1, 1939, resuming from Alexandra Palace on June 7, 1946. The first regular colour broadcasts didn't get broadcast until 1967.

The main broadcasters in the U.K. are British Broadcasting Corporation (BBC), ITV, Channel 4, Channel 5, Sky and S4C. These broadcasters have mainstream flagship channels and also cater for various target audiences by offering a choice of more specialist channels such as BBC4, ITVBe, More4. Some channels are now very much genre based. For example ITVBe tends to focus on celebrity lifestyle and reality television, whereas 5 U.S.A. focuses on American television drama and films.

Since 2012, all terrestrial TV channels in the U.K. have been digital. These channels are available on Freeview, which the British can connect to easily via aerial at home. In order to do this, a modern TV with digital capabilities is needed. However, if you only have an older TV, you can still pick up a set-top Freeview transmitter that can be connected to the aeria. The Freesat, a similar service accessed via satellite is also a good choice.

(1) TV License

The U.K. operates a TV licensing system to fund its public broadcasters, including the BBC. The license fee is applicable to anyone who wants to watch live TV in the U.K., whether via Freeview or one of the country's many satellite and cable operators.

An annual license can be bought online, with the license then either mailed or emailed to you. The license fee increases annually with inflation. The cost of a license for a color TV in the U.K. is £ 157.50. A license for a black and white TV is significantly cheaper, at £ 53. If visually-impaired, people can apply for a 50% discount on the license fee. Those aged 75 and over are currently exempt from TV license fees, although this is set to change in July 2020. If a person is caught watching live television without purchasing a license, he could be liable for a fine of up to £ 1,000.

(2) BBC

British Broadcasting Corporation (BBC), publicly financed broadcasting system in Great Britain, operating under royal charter. It held a monopoly on television in Great Britain from its introduction until 1954 and on radio until 1972. Headquarters are located in the Greater London borough of Westminster. It was established in 1922 as a private corporation. In 1925, upon recommendation of a parliamentary committee, the company was liquidated and replaced in 1927 by a public corporation, the British Broadcasting Corporation.

During World War II, British television service was interrupted but resumed in 1946. The BBC established its second channel in 1964, and it introduced the first regular colour television service in Europe in 1967. It retained its monopoly of television service in Britain until the passage of the *Television Act* of 1954. BBC's radio monopoly ended with the government's decision to permit, starting in the early 1970s, local commercial broadcasts. By the early 21st century BBC World Service broadcast in more than 40 languages to roughly 120 million people worldwide. World Service Television began broadcasting in 1991 and unveiled a 24-hour news channel, BBC News 24, in 1997.

BBC offers five radio networks in Britain, ranging from popular music to

Monopoly *vt.* 垄断
Headquarters *n.* 总部
Liquidate *vt.* 变卖

BBC Broadcasting House (from Londontopia)

news and information services, as well as national television channels. Under its charter the BBC may not advertise or broadcast sponsored programs. It is required to refrain from broadcasting any opinion of its own on current affairs and matters of public policy and to be impartial in its treatment of controversy.

III. Value and Attitudes

Impartial *a.* 中立的
Crack a quip 讲俏皮话
Quirky *a.* 古怪的
Bemuse *vt.* 使困惑

1. Mutual Respect and Tolerance of Different Faiths and Beliefs

The U.K. is one of the most tolerant societies in the world, with people being open to the inclusion of all without emphasis on their ethnic background, sexual orientation or place of origin. Although levels with diversity vary in different parts of the country, you don't need to be in London to feel the tolerance and respect that British people have for others. They understand that people all don't share the same beliefs and values and respect those values, ideas and beliefs of others whilst not imposing their own onto them.

2. Humour

Perhaps the most distinguishing part of the British character is humour. British people are the masters of jokes and satire, and everyone from cab drivers to Prince Charles are known for cracking a good quip or two. Humour is a great part about British attitudes and culture because it helps put people at ease and also to help them feel part of the society.

3. Tradition

The strange and quirky traditions are often things that British people take for granted but serve to delight and bemuse the international visitors. Whether it is their love of the Queen or their need for a Sunday Roast, traditions are what make Britain interesting. But it does not mean the British are not willing to incorporate the new. They respect the past at the same time embracing change, meaning even the oldest of universities retain their old-style charm while still being excellent modern institutions.

4. The Rule of Laws

The importance of law and rules should be referred to and reinforced to teach students to distinguish between right and wrong. This will teach children to take responsibility for their own actions. Students should be taught the reasons behind rules and laws, how they govern and protect us, and the consequences of what happens when these laws are broken.

Ⅳ. Marriage

In England and Wales people cannot marry if they are aged 16 or 17 and do not have parental consent. In Scotland both parties must be at least 16 years of age (parental consent is not required). The average British couple will be in a relationship for multiple years and live together before getting married. This varies significantly between individual circumstances and family backgrounds. The average age of (first) marriage is 33 for men and 30 for women. Almost half of British marriages end in divorce. In the past, people got married and stayed married. Divorce was very difficult, expensive and took a long time. Today, people's views on marriage are changing. Many couples, mostly in their twenties or thirties, live together (cohabit) without getting married. Only about 60% of these couples will eventually get married. People are generally getting married at a later age now and many women do not want to have children immediately. They prefer to concentrate on their jobs and put off having a baby until late thirties.

Here are some old British wedding traditions:

1. The White Dress

Bride *n.* 新娘
Groom *n.* 新郎
Gown *n.* 长服、礼服
Ward off 避开
Fertility *n.* 生育力
Confetti *n.* 五彩纸屑
Host *n.* 男主人

Historically, brides used to wear the best clothes they had, and they could be any colour — even black. It wasn't until Queen Victoria married Prince Albert in an ivory-white gown in 1840 that white became a fashionable wedding dress colour.

2. "Old, New, Borrowed, Blue"

This fun tradition is based on an old rhyme by an unknown English poet: "Something old, something new, something borrowed, something blue, and a silver sixpence in her shoe. " The old represents the past, new stands for the future. Borrowed refers to the happiness given to the bride by the new husband. Blue colour was believed to ward off evil. Nowadays, the final line about the sixpence is often not quoted. But as you may have guessed, it refers to wealth.

3. Throwing Rice

This joyful wedding custom has its roots in ancient Rome. Throwing grains of wheat or oats at newlyweds was thought to bring them fertility and wealth. These days, many people prefer confetti, because it's available in many colours and doesn't hurt when its thrown at you.

4. The First Dance

In the grand old days of royal balls, the first dance was normally the "opening number" that kicked off the party. It was customary for a male guest of honor to invite the lady of the house to join him in the first dance. This tradition subsequently became a wedding custom. The host, usually the bride's father, would dance with her first, followed by the groom.

5. The Honeymoon

Surprisingly, the romantic idea of a honeymoon is attributed to the most feisty and war-loving of all people, the Vikings. Newlywed Viking couples were sent to live in a cave for one month. Every day, a family member would visit them and bring them honeyed wine. That's where the name "honeymoon" comes from.

Feisty *a.* 精力充沛的
Threshold *n.* 门槛
Stumble *v.* 磕绊
Nuclear family 核心家庭
Extended family 几代同堂的大家庭
Archetypical *a.* 原型的

6. Carrying the Bride over the Threshold

Carrying the bride over the threshold in the U.K. started out as a way to protect the bride from evil spirits and prevent the bride from stumbling in her dress. It is a tradition that the groom carries his bride over the threshold of their new home, which symbolizes entering into a new life together.

This tradition is still alive in some places, but it has also evolved into an act of protection and love instead of just practicality. The groom carries the bride over the threshold, as a symbolic gesture of being strong enough for her in this moment and in all moments that may come. Moreover, by carrying his wife over the threshold, the groom is showing his appreciation for her, his acceptance of her as his wife, and taking responsibility for the bride.

V. Family

The average British family has classically been understood as a nuclear family with the extended family living separately. However, today the archetypical family (husband, wife and children) can no longer be the exact social expectation as divorce, remarriage, cohabitation of couples and births outside of marriage have become more common. According to national statistics, more children are being raised in single parent households, from 18 to 29 per cent between 1971 and 2002. By the year 2020, it is estimated that there will be more single people than married people. Some women are also choosing to have children as lone parents without being married.

The preference for most British families is to have a small family unit. This allows mobility and relieves economic pressure over a parent's lifetime. Parents often make strategic choices about their children's education to secure a good economic future for them. Children are encouraged to be independent and self-reliant at an early age. However, more adult children are living with their parents for economic reasons than ever before.

The average ages at which family life-events occur (e. g. marriage, children, retirement) are rising. This reflects the growing individualist orientation of both men and women — particularly of the middle class — to want to establish a career for themselves and travel before starting a family.

Pension *n.* 退休金　The state pension is granted at 67 for men and 65 for women. However, it is now common for people to work later into life and remain in the British workforce for several more years after the age of retirement.

Hippies

During the 1960s and 1970s, of a countercultural movement that rejected the mores of mainstream American life. The movement originated on college campuses in the America, although it spread to other countries, including Canada and the U.K. The name derived from "hip", a term applied to the Beats of the 1950s, such as Allen Ginsberg and Jack Kerouac, who were generally considered to be the precursors of hippies. Although the movement arose in part as opposition to U.S. involvement in the Vietnam War (1955-1975), hippies were often not directly engaged in politics, as opposed to their activist counterparts known as "Yippies" (Youth International Party).

Hippies were largely a white, middle-class group of teenagers and twenty somethings who belonged to what demographers call the baby-boom generation. They felt alienated from middle-class society, which they saw as dominated by materialism and repression. Hippies developed their own distinctive lifestyle, whereby they constructed a sense of marginality. Hippies were also known for their unique style, favouring long hair and casual, often unconventional, dress, sometimes in "psychedelic" colours. Many males grew beards, and both men and women wore sandals and beads. Long flowing so-called granny dresses were popular with women, and rimless granny glasses with both men and women. Hippies tended to be dropouts from society, forgoing regular jobs and careers, although some developed small businesses that catered to other hippies.

Demographer *n.* 人口统计学家
Alienated *a.* 疏远的、格格不入的
Repression *n.* 压制、压抑
Marginality *n.* 边缘化
Psychedelic *a.* 迷幻的
Rimless *a.* 无框的
Dropout *n.* 逃避现实社会的人
Forgo *vt.* 放弃
Cater to/for 迎合

VI. Leisure Time

Free time is important to the British, with most of the public taking part in some form of hobby or leisure activity. Popular activities include watching TV, eating out, and spending time with friends and family. Over half of British consumers went on nights out at least once a week in 2019, including

Hippie Style (from Love to Know)

to pubs and clubs. Some interests, such as gardening, are much more popular with older generations than young people.

1. Gardening

Gardening has been a popular pastime in the United Kingdom since Roman Times. Not only do people practice it as a hobby and visit public gardens, but they also open their private gardens up to the public for visitation. Over two-thirds of British adults visit a garden centre every year. What's more, most people have a garden on their property. Every town in Britain has one or more DIY (Do It Yourself) centres and garden centres. These are like supermarkets for the home and garden and are very popular with British home-owners at the weekends.

Gardening became particularly important to those during the coronavirus pandemic when lockdowns caused many to have to stay at home with limited access to leisure activities. A survey in 2020 found that the majority stated that gardening " helped relieve stress and anxiety, contributing to the mental wellbeing". Therefore, it is unsurprising that annual expenditure on gardening, plants, and flowers in the U.K. showed year-over-year growth in 2020, accounting for approximately 6.2 billion British pounds.

The U.K. is home to some of the most glorious gardens in the world. From Kew Gardens in London to Stourhead in Wiltshire, people can journey through centuries of landscaping and admire impressive displays of topiary. Besides their own outdoor spaces, the British frequently visit public gardens and private gardens through the National Garden Scheme.

Households Gardens in the U.K. (from Wikipedia)

2. Museums and Theatres

(1) Museums

The number of the U.K. museums has exploded in recent decades, nearly doubling since the early 1970s. The U.K. Museums Association's 2014 Museums & Galleries Yearbook contains the most comprehensive catalogue of the U.K. museums, galleries, and historic properties, listing roughly 2,500 organizations. The U.K. museums receive over 100 million visits each year. More than half of the adult population in England (52%), two thirds of five to ten year olds, and 59% of eleven to fifteen year olds visited a U.K.

museum in 2009. The 350 museums in Scotland receive twenty-five million annual visits, and contribute over £ 800 m to Scotland's economy. Households in the highest ten percent of the disposable income decile group in the United Kingdomspent 0.8 percent of their weekly household expenditure on cinema, theatre, museum and other similar cultural/entertainment venues in the financial year ending 2020, which was the highest among the income groups.

British Museum

Archaeology *n.* 考古学
Ethnography *n.* 民族学
Marble *n.* 大理石
Accede *v.* 同意

British Museum is a comprehensive national museum with particularly outstanding holdings in archaeology and ethnography. It is located in the Bloomsbury district of the borough of Camden. Established by *The Act of Parliament* in 1753, the museum was originally based on three collections: those of Sir Hans Sloane; Robert Harley, 1st earl of Oxford; and Sir Robert Cotton. The collections were opened to the public in 1759.

Among the British Museum's most famous holdings are the Elgin Marbles, which were removed in the early 19th century from the Parthenon in Athens and shipped to England by arrangement of Thomas Bruce, 7th Lord Elgin. The Greek government frequently demanded the return of the marbles, but the British Museum did not accede, claiming that it had saved the marbles

The Great Court

from certain damage and deterioration, and the issue remained controversial. Other objects in the collection include Greek sculptures; the Rosetta Stone, which provided the key to reading ancient Egyptian hieroglyphs; exquisite gold, silver, and shell work from the ancient Mesopotamian City of Ur; treasure from the 7th-century-CE ship burial found at Sutton Hoo, Suffolk; and Chinese ceramics from the Ming and other dynasties.

Sculpture *n.* 雕塑
Hieroglyph *n.* 象形文字
Ceramic *n.* 陶瓷(品)
Patronage *n.* 资助、赞助、提携

(2) Theaters

Another hobby of the British is watching theater, which has a long history in the U.K. The Renaissance that had started in Europe as early as the 14th century had led to a new flourishing of arts and culture all over Europe. England began to see a growth of the arts in Tudor times, and Elizabeth encouraged this through her patronage of the theatre, music and art. Shakespeare began writing his plays during Elizabeth's reign, and a number of them had themes connected to English history. Purpose-built theatres were popular and offered tiered seating with prices suitable for people from all ranks of society. Many nobles protected groups of actors and became their patrons.

No trip to London's West End is complete without seeing a theatre show.

Royal Opera House

London has some of the best plays and musicals in the world, but there's so much more to this cultural district than neon lights and famous faces. The glamorous, buzzing West End we know and love today is at the heart of London's cultural scene. There's so much to see in London's West End. From world-class plays, to musicals, to comedies, dance shows and operas, there's something for everyone, at every budget.

The West End has some of the longest-running shows in the world. The top five longest-running West End musicals and plays which you can still see today are:

The Mousetrap at St. Martin's Theatre — 1974 to present

Les Misérables at Sondheim Theatre (originally Barbican Centre) — 1985 to present

The Phantom of the Opera at Her Majesty's Theatre — 1986 to present

The Woman in Black at Fortune Theatre — 1989 to present

Mamma Mia! at Novello Theatre (originally Prince of Wales Theatre) — 1999 to present

The Laurence Olivier Awards, or simply the Olivier Awards, are presented annually by the Society of London Theatre to recognize excellence in professional theatre in London at an annual ceremony in the capital. The Olivier Awards are recognized internationally as the highest honour in British theatre and are considered equivalent to Broadway's Tony Awards and France's Molière Award.

Britain's long-standing theatre culture has given birth to many famous playwrights like William Shakespeare, Oscar Wilde and so on. Here are some brief introduction to these playwrights:

William Shakespeare (April 26, 1564 - April 23, 1616), an English playwright, poet, and actor who is widely regarded as the greatest writer in the English language. He is also often called England's national poet. Many of his works have been translated into other languages and his plays continue to be produced till day. Popular during his lifetime, he acquired an iconic status after his death. Some of his most well-known works include: *Hamlet*,

Laurence Olivier in a Scene from *Hamlet*

Macbeth, *A Midsummer Night's Dream*, *Othello*, *Romeo and Juliet*.

Oscar Wilde was a flamboyant and vivacious playwright of the 19th century. He studied at Oxford and was a keen classicist. He wrote a number of great plays as well as essays, poetry and novels. His most famous play and the uncontested number one on this list, *The Important of Being Earnest* is a fantastic farcical comedy that simply must be read by any actor, playwright or decent human being. He is one of England's best playwrights.

3. Pubs

The word "pub" is short for public house. There are over 60,000 pubs in the U.K. (53,000 in England and Wales, 5,200 in Scotland and 1,600 in Northern Ireland). One of the oldest pubs, Fighting Cocks in St. Albans, Herts, is located in a building that dates back to the eleventh century. Pubs are major focal points of social life, formerly mainly for men, but increasingly for women. People talk, eat, drink, meet their friends and relax there. Pubs are open from Monday to Saturday from 11:00 A.M. to 11:00 P.M, and on Sunday, from noon to 10:30 P.M. or 11:00 P.M. Many pubs serve high-quality food and a variety of snacks at reasonable prices. Some pubs provide games for their customers' entertainment: perhaps a dart boards, a pool or billiards table, sets of dominoes, and other board games may be found, along with pinball and slot machines. Whether you are cheering on your favourite football team or are simply enjoying a few drinks with friends, a sports oriented pub is a great place to soak up the atmosphere and catch all the latest action.

4. Other Leisure Activities

The British spend much of their leisure time engaged in home-based activities:listening to music, watching television, playing video games, and gardening. According to the survey, conducted between April 2017 and March 2018, around 91 percent of 16 to 24 year olds spent some part of their free time listening to music. Making home improvements is a popular leisure activity as well as a money-saving practice. Many men spend their weekends angling, boating, bicycling, or tinkering with motorbikes and cars, repairing or working on their vehicles in the garage and backyard. The British love of animals is legendary, and many British families keep pets, such as dogs, cats, goldfish and parakeets.

VII. Sports

The U.K. is located in North Western Europe and is home to a very diverse range of sports. The lush geography has led to the development of football and rugby as national past times, while other sports are slowly gaining a footing. Sports and physical recreation have always been popular. Local governments provide cheap sport and leisure facilities such as swimming pools, tennis courts, parks and golf courses for residents. People go to watch other people play sports like football or take part in sports themselves.

Britain is home to several important international sports competitions. The Open Championship — also known, outside of Britain, as the British Open — is a golf tournament held annually, often at the world-renowned course at St. Andrews in Scotland. The All — England (Wimbledon) Championships is one of the world's leading tennis competitions. Celebrated horse-racing events include the Royal Ascot, the Derby, and the Grand National steeplechase. The Henley Royal Regatta is the world's premiere rowing championship.

Although the United Kingdom's climate often rewards staying indoors, the British are enthusiasts of outdoor leisure activities and are well served by an extensive network of hiking and bicycling paths, national parks, and other amenities. Especially popular are the Lake District, which preserves a scenic area commemorated in many works by English poets; the rugged Scottish Highlands and Inner Hebrides islands; and the mountainous Welsh region of Snowdonia National Park, a magnet for climbers from around the world.

1. Soccer

The modern game of football (soccer) is generally accepted to have originated in England. The game's first organization — the Football Association — was founded in England in 1863, and the first football match played between England and Scotland — the oldest rivalry in the sport — was at Glasgow in 1872. In 1966 England hosted and won the World Cup; it was the third host nation to win the championship.

In the U.K., the most popular league is known as the Premier League and consists of the 20 best teams from all over the U.K. The most popular of these teams are Manchester United, Liverpool and Arsenal. The two most famous Football Championships in the U.K. are the FA Cup and the Capital One Cup. There are 92 professional football clubs that participate in each of these tournaments each year.

2. Rugby and Cricket

Rugby and cricket have also long enjoyed great popularity in Britain. According to tradition, rugby began in 1823 at Rugby School in England. In 1871 the Rugby Football Union was formed as the English governing body, and the rival Rugby Football League was founded in 1895. The two are different in rules such as the number of players and in ways to advance the ball. England, Scotland, and Wales all have club competitions in both union and league versions of the game and national teams are also sent to the Six Nations Championship and to World Cup tournaments by the three regions.

Cricket is the national sport of the U.K. and became popular in the U.K. in the 17th century. Its origins may date to 13th-century England, and county competition in England was formally organized in the 19th century. Today there are 18 professional county clubs in the U.K. with all of them being named after historic counties. Each summer these county clubs participate in the First Class County Championship, which consists of two leagues of nice teams in which matches are played over four days. International matches, known as tests, began in 1877 with a match between England and Australia.

Cricket

3. Tennis

Tennis is growing not only as a participant sport but also as a spectator sport. Wimbledon is the most popular Tennis Tournament in the U.K. and has been played in England since 1877. Wimbledon is one of the four grand slam events on the ATP Tour which also includes the Australian Open, the U.S. Open and the French Open. The U.K. has many public facilities throughout which offer tennis at little to no cost for the general public.

VIII. Holidays

1. January: New Year's Day

On New Year's Eve (31 December), it's traditional to celebrate with friends and family, with a focus on the stroke of midnight. Festivities take place across the four nations, with Edinburgh's "Hogmanay" being one of the greatest outdoor celebrations of New Year's Eve in the world. New Year's Day (1 January) is a public holiday and the celebrations will last well into the night, or — in many cases — the morning.

2. 14 February: Valentine's Day

Although there is not a bank holiday to mark this day, people can feel its presence in the lead up with shop fronts being lined with red roses, bouquets of flowers, chocolates, teddy bears and Valentine's cards. It's common for couples to exchange gifts and go out for dinner together.

3. 17 March: Saint Patrick's Day

It is celebrated by Irish communities and many others around the world. Many U.K. cities host their own official Saint Patrick's Day celebrations, while many people choose to celebrate instead in venues around where they live or even throw parties at home. Dressing up in green, grabbing a pint of

Guinness and heading out are the best ways to join in the celebrations.

4. March-April: Easter

Each year the Easter weekend falls on a different date-any time between March 22 and April 25 — as it depends on the moon. In the U.K. there are two bank holidays to mark Easter: Good Friday and Easter Monday. This Christian holiday is traditionally celebrated with a sit-down meal (usually among family or friends) to mark the beginning of spring.

Another tradition that people, regardless of their faith or background, tend to enjoy is the Easter eggs, which are usually made of chocolate and appear on supermarket shelves in the lead-up to Easter. They range from tiny ones that are perfect for hiding in the garden, balcony, or home, to eggs the size of the head.

5. 31 October: Halloween

Halloween or Hallowe'en (short for All Hallows' evening) is a celebration observed in many countries around the world. Many say that Halloween traditions were influenced by Celtic harvest festivals and the modern way of celebrating it is increasing in the U.K.

Activities like guising (trick-or-treating), pumpkin carving, lighting bonfires, apple bobbing and telling or watching scary stories are traditions for this holiday. If you live in rented accommodation, don't be surprised if small groups of children turn up at your door in monster or ghost costumes looking for sweets. Adults in the U.K. also tend to enjoy Halloween as an excuse to hold fancy-dress (costume) parties.

6. 25 and 26 December: Christmas Day and Boxing Day

Christmas is one of the biggest annual celebrations in the U.K., and the festivities are not limited to one day. In fact, the build-up to Christmas starts weeks before the day itself with Christmas trees, markets, gift-giving and the consumption of the U.K.'s traditional mince pies (and cream, sometimes) taking centre stage throughout most of the month of December. It traditionally celebrates Jesus Christ's birth but many aspects of this holiday have pagan origins. Christmas is a time for many people to give and receive gifts and prepare special festive meals.

Boxing Day is a holiday celebrated after Christmas Day, occurring on the second day of Christmastide (26 December). Though it originated as a holiday to give gifts to the poor, today Boxing Day is primarily known as a shopping holiday. It originated in Great Britain and is celebrated in a number of countries that previously formed part of the British Empire.

Part Two   The United States of America

Chapter 1   Land and Cities

Think and Explore

What are the geographic features of the U.S.A.?

How does the geographic features influence the water system?

Find out factors which affect the rising and flourishing of cities.

I. Location and Size

The United States of America is located in the central part of North America with its two youngest states — Alaska in the northwestern part of North America and Hawaii in the central Pacific. The continental United States stretches from the Atlantic Ocean on the east to the Pacific Ocean on the west (Continental U.S. includes 4 time zones). It is bounded by Canada on the north and by Mexico and the Gulf of Mexico on the south.

The border with Canada, some 6,000 km long, runs along the 49th parallel in the west and then through four of the five Great Lakes, ending at the Atlantic Coast. The boundary is open and undefended. The border with Mexico, about 3,000 km long, starts from the mouth of the Rio Grande River, through the lower reaches of the river and finally ends at the Pacific Seashore. U.S. has established numerous checkpoints along it.

It stretches about 4,500 km from the western coastline to the eastern, and 2,500 km from the south to the north. The total area is 9,629,091 km^2, of which the land covers 9,158,960 km^2 and the water 470,131 km^2. Considering only land area, the United States is third in size behind Russia

Bound *vt.* 形成……
的边界
Border *n.* 边境
Undefended *a.* 无人
防守的
Checkpoint *n.* 检查站

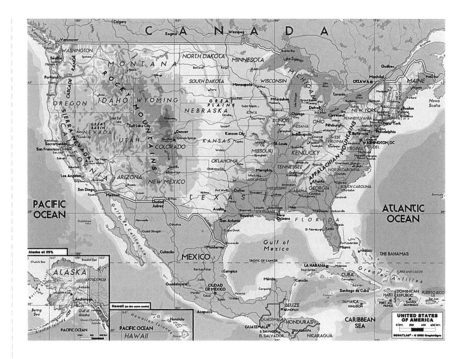

and China, just ahead of Canada.

The long coastline provides favorable conditions for foreign trade and the fishing industry, and also brings much influence of the oceanic air mass. Lying within the northern temperate zone, it grows rich agricultural products.

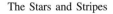

The Stars and Stripes   Great Seal of the United States

II. Geographical Features and Climate

America has varied geographical features, large mountains, a vast central plain, a dry desert, low-lying basins, rugged mountains and broad river valleys. It can be divided into three distinctive areas according to their geographical features: the eastern part, the western part and the Great Plains in between.

The eastern part consists of the highlands formed by the Appalachian Range. It takes up 1/6 of the continental American territory. These highlands are relatively low, with an average altitude of 800 meters above sea level. The highest mountain in it is **Mount Mitchell** (2,037 m). To the east of Appalachian Range is the narrow Atlantic Coastal Plain. Dairy farming is the most important farm activity. New England lies in the northeastern part, which is regarded as the cradle of America not only for a number of world-famous universities, such as Harvard there but also for the Boston Tea Party and the first gunfire from Lexington.

The western part consists of high plateaus and mountains, which extend from the border of Canada to that of Mexico. It holds one-third of the country's continental territory. The Rocky Mountains are spectacular with national and state parks dotting here and there. The Rockies rise over 3,000 meters above sea level and form the Continental Divide. To the west of it are the two plateaus: Columbia Plateau in the north and Colorado Plateau in the south, with the Great Basin in between. The best known of Columbia Plateau

Plateau *n.* 高原
Territory *n.* 领土

is the Grand Canyon of the Colorado River, with a maximum depth of 1,800 meters. Death Valley in Eastern California is the lowest point in the North America while Mountain Whitney(4,418m) is the highest peak in the U.S. outside Alaska. Along the Rockies, rivers flow either westward or eastward. Few of rivers in the Great Basin find outlets to the sea, and most of them are shallow and salty. Owing to the hot and dry climate, the evaporation is huge. Thus some salt lakes are generated. The Great Salt Lake in Utah is the most famous. Along the Pacific Coast are the lower and gentler Coast Ranges which include many forested hills and lowlands. Owing to the abundant sunshine there, large amounts of fresh fruits produced here are shipped to markets in America and Asia.

The central part lies the vast Great Plains between the Appalachian Range and the Rocky Mountains. Through the center of this vast land runs the mighty Mississippi River. The sediment of the rivers makes the soil of the basin rich. The large size and rich soil provide good conditions for developing agriculture and have made this region the "Barn of America". The central plains stretch from the Great Lakes in the north to the Gulf of Mexico in the south with the Rockies and the Appalachians on either side. It looks like a trumpet and creates good geographical conditions for the cold air from the north and the warm air from the south to go smoothly into the inner part of the land. This explains the disasters caused by the hurricanes and the like. In the west part of the central plain, getting less rainfall as it extends westward to the Rockies, lies the great prairies. Today the area is still a cattle country. Moreover, much of the nations' wheat is grown here. So this area is also known as the "breadbasket" of America.

The United States is mainly situated in the northern temperature zone, with some mild subtropic area. Influenced by such factors as location (latitude and altitude), distance from oceans, and prevailing winds, the U.S. climate varies from extremely cold in northern Alaska to semitropical in southern Florida and Hawaii. Between these extremes are many kinds of climate.

New England is dominated by the maritime climate with four distinctive

Evaporation *n.* 蒸发
Sediment *n.* 沉积物
Barn *n.* 粮仓
Trumpet *n.* 喇叭
Disaster *n.* 灾难
Hurricane *n.* 飓风
Subtropic *n.* 亚热带
Prevailing wind 盛行风

Tip21 结合美国地理位置、地形、气候、水系,理解其产业、城市、和人口分布特征。为何纽约能成为全美最大城市和经济中心? 为何芝加哥能成为美国中西部中心城市和陆路交通枢纽?

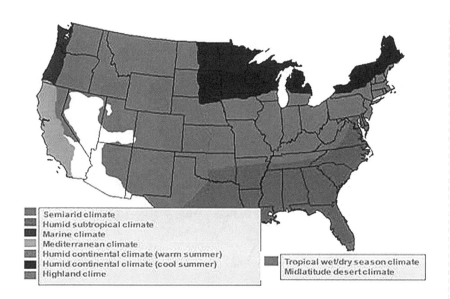

seasons. The climate is temperate, with long cold winters, and short and warm summers. The region receives plenty of rainfall.

The climate of the Midwest is temperate too. However, the lay of land gives north and south winds free access, sometimes resulting in sharp changes in temperature and other disasters. As for the pacific coast, affected by prevailing westerly winds that blow from the Pacific, a mild and humid climate runs through the year.

The South is blessed with plentiful rainfall and a mild climate. The frost-free period last at least for six months of the year. Crops and plants grow easily and fast there.

III. Water System

Surrounded by oceans in the east, south and west, five lakes lying in the north, and the Mississippi River running through the central plains, the U.S. has rich water resources.

The Mississippi River, the most important and longest river in North America, flows from north Minnesota to the Gulf of Mexico, with a length of 3,780 kilometers and a drainage area of over 3 million square kilometers. Nearly all the rivers west of the Appalachians and east of the Rockies flow into each other and empty into the Mississippi River. It is known as "the father of waters" in America. St. Louise is an important city by the

Drainage *n.* 排水 (系统)

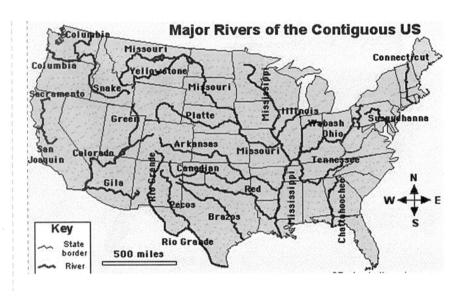

Mississippi River in the Midwest.

The Great Lakes are composed of five lakes: Lake Michigan, Lake Superior, Lake Erie, Lake Huron and Lake Ontario. They are the largest lake group in the world and contain about half of the world's fresh water. Among the five lakes, only Lake Michigan belongs to the U.S. completely. Lake Superior ($82,414 \text{ km}^2$), is the largest freshwater lake (by surface area) in the world. The famous Niagara Falls is located between Lake Erie and Lake Ontario. The width of the Falls is about 1,240 meters and the drop averages 49 meters. All the five lakes are inter-connected, reaching the Atlantic by way of the St. Lawrence River. They are linked to many inland industrial cities

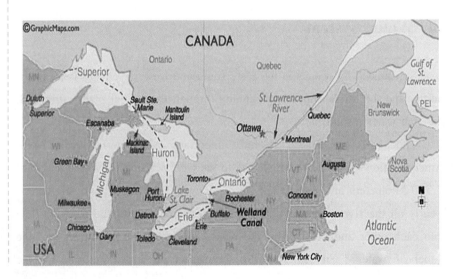

through rivers and canals and play an extremely important role in the transportation. Along the lakes are situated major industrial cities like Chicago, Detroit, Cleveland and Buffalo.

Other rivers like Hudson River, Potomac River are also important because these rivers run through the cities, not only offering large quantity of fresh water but also providing economic means of transportation to connect the cities with other areas.

Ⅳ. Natural Resources

The United States is a land rich in natural resources, such as land, water, natural gas, coal, oil, are especially plentiful. America has plenty of fertile soil. Farmlands in the country make up about 12% of the arable lands in the world. America is rich in water resources. America as a whole has little trouble with shortage of fresh water. About one-third of America is covered with forests. The greatest virgin forests are in the northwestern states of Washington and Oregon.

The United States is also rich in mineral resources. It ranks among the countries with the greatest reserves of coal, iron ore and oil. It also abounds in lead, copper, zinc, gold, and aluminum.

Coal deposits are widely distributed in the U.S., and most coal reserves are to be found in the Appalachians, the Central Plain, and the Rockies. Coal is mainly used to generate electricity and produce steel, as well as chemicals.

In addition to coal, America also has major oil shale and oil sand deposits. America was once the largest oil-producing country in the world. Most of the oil reserves are along the coast of the Gulf of Mexico. Texas, Louisiana, and Oklahoma produce more than half of the country's total. Alaska is also rich in oil. The production, processing and marketing of petroleum products make up one of America's large industries.

America was once rich in gold and silver. In 1848, gold was discovered in California and caused what has been known in American history as the Gold Rush.

V. Principal Cities and Landmarks

Washington, the capital of the U.S.A., is in Washington D. C. which is directly governed by the federal government. Situated on the Potomac River, it covers 158 square kilometers and has a population of 705,749 (2019). The city is named after the first American President George Washington. It hosts the headquarters of all the branches of the American federal system. Apart from being a political center, it is also a cultural one. Except for White House, the Capitol, there are numerous museums, theatres and other places of interest such as Washington Monument, Lincoln Memorial, Jefferson Memorial, and the Library of Congress, the National Air and Space Museum, the Smithsonian Institute, etc. The city has little heavy industry, and its residents are mainly engaged in light and service industries to meet the needs of the federal government and cultural institutions.

New York City is the largest city with a population of over 8 million, and the commercial and financial center in the United States. The city consists of 5 boroughs which include Manhattan, Brooklyn, Queens, Bronx and Staten Island. Manhattan is not only a financial but also an entertainment center. Broadway, Times Square, Wall Street, Fifth Avenue and Central Park are there. The headquarters of the United Nations is also located in Manhattan. The Statue of Liberty, a gift from France in 1886, standing at the gate of New York Harbor, is the symbol of America. New York Harbor is the chief port at the mouth of the Hudson River.

Los Angeles, a seaport and the second largest city in America, spreading far and wide. It is an important electronic center. Silicon Valley and Standford University are not far from it. As the major seaport along the west pacific coast, it also plays an important role in shipping, automobile, and communications industry. It leads the country in atomic research and the manufacture of aircrafts and parts. Hollywood, located in Los Angeles, is regarded as the heart of motion picture and movie industry.

Chicago, the third largest city and "the Windy City", lies on the southwest shore of Lake Michigan. The advantageous location has made it the main connection between the east and the west ever since it is founded in the early 1800s. The city is one of the country's leading industrial cities where both heavy and light industries are highly developed. It is the predominant trading center of agricultural goods in America. As the chief railway center in America, with the biggest airport hub in the Midwest and a harbor open to ocean traffic by the St. Lawrence Seaway, Chicago is considered as an industrial, commercial, financial and transportation center in the Midwest Region. Chicago is also a cultural center, for it has one of the world's best collections of modern architecture and is regarded as Exhibition Hall of Architecture, such as the 110-storey Willis Tower and the Art Institute of Chicago.

◎ Exercises

I. Choose the best answer from the four choices.

1. The continental United States is situated in the _____ part of North America.

    A. northern   B. southern

    C. central   D. eastern

2. The United States is the _____ largest country in the world in terms of land area.

    A. third   B. fourth

    C. fifth   D. sixth

3. _____ is the largest state of the United States in land area.

    A. California   B. Texas

    C. Alaska   D. Pennsylvania

4. The _____ Mountains form the continental divide of the United States.

    A. Appalachian   B. Rocky

    C. Sierra Nevada   D. Cordillera

5. The highest peak in the continental United States is in the _____ Mountain Ranges.

    A. Rocky   B. Sierra

    C. Appalachian   D. Cascade

6. Alaska was bought by the United States from _____ in 1867.

    A. Canada   B. France

    C. Germany   D. Russia

7. The international rivers of the United States do NOT include the _____ River.

    A. St. Lawrence   B. Rio Grande

    C. Columbia   D. Mississippi

8. The _____ River flows through New York City.

    A. Missouri   B. St. Lawrence

    C. Colorado   D. Hudson

9. Of the five Great Lakes, Lake _____ is wholly within the U.S.

    A. Superior   B. Michigan

    C. Huron   D. Erie

10. Niagara Falls is located on the U.S.-Canadian border between _____.

    A. Lake Michigan and Lake Huron   B. Lake Huron and Lake Erie

    C. Lake Erie and Lake Ontario   D. Lake Superior and Lake Michigan

11. Southern Florida has a _____ climate.

    A. cold   B. tropical

    C. temperate   D. semitropical

12. The Midwest of the United States has _____ climate.

    A. cold   B. warm

    C. dry   D. temperate

13. The Rockies are cooler or colder than other regions in the same latitude because of their _____.

    A. high latitude   B. high altitude

    C. longitude   D. distance from the ocean

14. Which of the following is NOT in Washington D.C.?

    A. The U.S. Capitol.   B. The White House.

    C. The Pentagon Building.   D. The UN Headquarters.

II. Fill in the blanks.

1. Columbus discovered the New World in the year of _____.

2. The English king claimed the territory of North America based on the voyage of _____.

3. The first permanent settlement in North America was established in today's _____ in the year of _____.

4. New England was founded by a group of religious believers called _____.

5. Pennsylvania was planted by _____ who was a _____ in religion.

III. Match the names of the cities in Column A with their features in Column B.

Column A

Column B

1. (   ) Washington D.C.   A. the third-largest city in the U.S.

2. (   ) New York   B. the movie center and the 2nd-largest city of U.S.

3. (   ) Chicago   C. the seat of the Federal Government

4. (   ) Los Angeles   D. the largest city in the U.S.

5. (   ) Philadelphia   E. the"Space City, U.S.A."

6. (   ) Detroit   F. the largest leather, shoe and wool market

7. (   ) Houston   G. the seat of the Continental Congress

8. (   ) San Francisco   H. the"Motor City, U.S.A."

9. (   ) Boston   I. one of American's top steel-making area

10. (   ) Pittsburgh   J. the city that has the largest Chinatown

IV. Give brief answers to the following questions.

1. What are the factors that affect the climate of the U.S.A.?

2. How is the American population distributed?

Chapter 2　History

Think and Explore

Why is American Independence War also called American Revolution?

What is the significance of American Civil War? Can it be avoided?

How does the Westward Movement affect American national character?

How does the United States rise up from the two world wars?

Ⅰ. Period of Local Indians

Inhabit *vt.* 居住
Navigator *n.* 航海者
Tip22　欧洲移民是
如何对待北美印第安
土著居民的?

Before the Europeans arrived and settled down in North America, the land was inhabited by the Indians, who were believed descendants of Mongoloid people. They may come from Asia forty and fifty thousand years ago.

Christopher Columbus, was believed to be the first to discover America in 1492 when he sailed west from Portugal to find a sea trade route to India. Believing he had reached India, Columbus called the native people Indians. That's why Native Americans are also called American Indians. Following his footsteps, Amerigo Vespucci, an Italian navigator discovered the South America. The newly-found continent was later named after him and known as America.

It was estimated at least 5 million Indians living there before the Discovery. Native Americans were hunters and gradually developed into many tribes, such as Apache and Hopi in the southwest, Eskimo in the north, Cherokee and Creek in the southeast. Nowadays, there are about 250,000

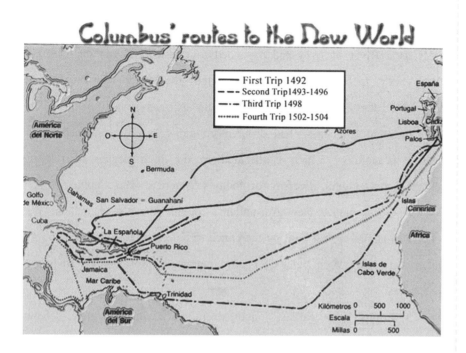

Indians living in North America.

II. Colonial Period

Many European countries established colonies in North America from the 16th century to the 18th century. The major colonies were controlled by Spain, the Netherlands, France and Britain.

In the early 16th century, Spain explored and conquered most of South America (except Brazil), Central America, and the southern part of North America from Florida to California. The Spanish came for 3 Gs — gold (to get rich), God (to spread Catholicism) and glory (to serve the king). The Spanish exploited the Indians mercilessly, enslaving them in gold and silver mines where many died or became disabled. Spanish ruling continued for centuries. Today, strong Spanish cultural influences can be still seen in those areas.

The great wealth from American colonies attracted other European powers. The Dutch, the French, and the English followed, explored and established colonies in different parts of North America.

The Dutch had good vision. They set up the settlement at the mouth of the Hudson River in 1624 and expanded to Connecticut and the Delaware River Valley. In New Netherland, the Dutch, the French, the Swedes, the Portuguese, the Finns, the English and the Africans lived together. They spoke different languages, had different religions, yet they learned to live together peacefully, which contributed to the high degree of religious tolerance and cultural diversity of today's America. The Capital of New Netherland was named New Amsterdam, roughly today's Manhattan. Wall Street was at first a wall built by the Dutch to defend against the Indians. The Dutch also set up West India Company, conducted profitable fur trade with local tribes.

The English were jealous, fought several wars with the Dutch, defeated them in 1675 and took over the colony. New Netherland was renamed New York in honor of its owner, the then duke of York, the king's brother and heir to the English throne.

In 1530s, Frenchman Jacques Cartier explored the St. Lawrence River. In 1604, the French built small settlements along the river and founded Montreal and Quebec in Canada. It was during the rule of King Louis XIV (1643-1715) that the French colonies became powerful. They claimed French ownership of Canada and the Great Lakes region. As they traveled down the Mississippi River, they started the city of St. Louis and New Orleans, farther down. In the 1680s, the French explored the vast territory watered by the Mississippi and the Missouri Rivers and then built forts and missions through the Mississippi River Valley. The vast region controlled by the French was named Louisiana. The establishment of New France incited action from Britain.

Fort *n.* 堡垒、要塞
Incite *vt.* 煽动
Persecution *n.* 迫害
Pilgrim *n.* 朝圣者

The first British colony — Virginia — was established in 1607. The second colony — Plymouth — was established by separatist Puritans from religious persecution in Britain. In 1620, 102 Puritan pilgrims boarded a ship called the Mayflower and sailed for the New World. The strong wind brought them further north of the planned destination. Believing themselves outside the rule of any government, the male passengers signed an agreement, *The Mayflower Compact*, to build a self-ruling society — the Puritans agreed to abide by the just and equal laws drafted by their chosen leaders. The pilgrims had a hard time in the first winter. Almost half of them died of hunger and cold. They learned to plant corn with the help of local American Indians and had a good harvest the following autumn. They had a big celebration to thank God in November. That's how Thanksgiving Day came into being and it was later made a national holiday.

Destination *n.* 目的地
Compact *n.* 协约
Self-ruling *a.* 自治的
Abide by 遵从
Pious *a.* 虔诚的

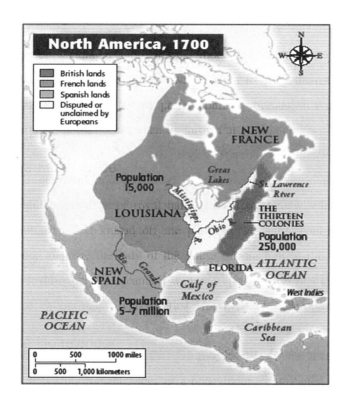

The thirteen colonies were generally grouped as the New England colonies, the Middle colonies and the Southern colonies according to their locations. The New England colonies were mainly inhabited by Puritans. Puritans in New England were pious and strictly followed the *Bible* for religion guidance. Therefore they attached great importance to education so people could read the *Bible* directly. Massachusetts was the first colony to make a law that villages with over fifty families must build a school supported by tax. The practice was followed by other New England colonies. Many well-known universities are located in today's New England, such as Harvard, Yale, MIT, Brown, Dartmouth, to name a few, the highest concentration of well-known top 40 universities in the world.

Diversified *a.* 多元的
Guarantee *vt.* 确保
Autonomy *n.* 自主、自治
Tip23 为什么说"五月花号契约"是美国精神的源头？它体现了哪些原则？

The Middle colonies include New Jersey, New York, Pennsylvania, Delaware and Maryland. Here, the societies were more diversified, cosmopolitan and tolerant than in New England. William Penn, founder of Pennsylvania, contributed a lot to the success of the colony. He advocated and guaranteed religious freedom, free and fair trial by jury, freedom from unjust imprisonment and free elections. New York, New Jersey and Delaware, formerly belonged to New Netherland, were later conceded to England when the Dutch were defeated by the English in 1664. Maryland was founded by Lord Baltimore who wanted to build a colony for Catholics because they were persecuted in England. Protestants also came and a law was passed to grant religious freedom to all Christians in 1649.

The southern colonies consist of Virginia, North and South Carolina and Georgia. They were mostly rural, favorable for farming. Grain, tobacco, cotton were the main produce. Colonial farming involved intensive labor and the immigrant nobles were too proud to work the land, so they bought African Negro slaves to work for them. Most of the colonial Negro slaves lived in the south engaging in farming.

III. American Revolution

Ties between the colonies and their mother country were good before the Seven Years War (1756-1763) ended. The American colonists needed the British protection against possible attacks. The thirteen colonies had long enjoyed high degrees of autonomy, liberties and democracy unseen in other European colonies. Things began to change after the Seven Years War.

In 1763, Britain won the Seven Years War but the war debts ran high. To pay off its debts and reduce its economic burden, the British government began to increase the economic exploitation of the colonies. A number of taxes were imposed on colonies and soldiers were sent to enforce their collection. Having been used to self-rule, colonists claimed that only their elected representatives could impose tax on them, not the British Parliament in which they had not representation. The colonists protested by boycotting British goods and some other measures.

In 1765 the British Parliament passed the *Stamp Act* to raise money to pay for the defense of colonies. In Boston and some other cities angry mobs attacked government officials selling stamps. Merchants and Shopkeepers refused to sell British goods. Consumers refused to buy British goods and began to produce home-made products to replace British imports. After several years of colonial resistance and under the pressure of British merchants who had suffered from the boycott, the British parliament repealed the taxes except on tea as a symbol of authority. The colonists won a major concession.

Some colonists were more radical because they favored independence from Britain. And those colonists were not content and still resisted the tax on tea. Their final goal was to seek independence from Britain and they were waiting for a chance to break away from Britain. At this time, the British East India Company, which brought a lot of profits to the British government, had trouble selling its tea stored in warehouses in large quantities. To help the company out of difficulty, the British parliament allowed it to undersell the tea in its American colonies without paying tax. *The Act* harmed the interests of local tea merchants. The radical colonists took advantage of the situation. On December 16, 1773, 60 colonists disguised as Indians, boarded on the tea ship and poured the tea into the sea. The event is known as the Boston Tea Party.

Colonists feared that the British Parliament would also violate their interests and liberties one day. The colonists decided to act together to defend their interests and liberties. Each colony sent their delegates to Philadelphia to find a solution in 1774. The event is known as the First Continental Congress. As things went on, they were gradually determined to take up arms to defend their rights and liberty. On April 19, 1775, the British general learned that

Boycott *vt.* 抵制
Mob *n.* 暴民
Stamp *n.* 印花税
Warehouse *n.* 仓库
Disguise *vt.* 伪装
Violate *vt.* 侵犯

Militiamen *n.* 民兵
Weapon *n.* 武器
Disarm *v.* 缴械
Provisional *a.* 临时的

militiamen were collecting weapons in Lexington, Massachusetts and sent several hundred soldiers to disarm them. Gun shooting broke out between them and grew into serious military clashes. Thus the armed struggle for American independence began. In May 1775, the Second Continental Congress was held in Philadelphia and acted as a provisional government of the 13 colony-states. Colonist delegates voted to break away from Britain. It established the Continental Army and Navy under the command of George Washington. Thomas Jefferson drafted *The Declaration of Independence*, which Karl Marx commented "the first declaration of the rights of the individuals" and was adopted by the Second Continental Congress on July 4, 1776.

The Declaration presented a public defense of the American War of Independence, and most importantly, it explained the philosophy behind the war, that men have a natural right to "Life, Liberty and the Pursuit of Happiness", that government can rule only with "the consent of the governed", that any government may be dissolved when it fails to protect the rights of the people. This theory of politics and guiding principles borrowed a lot from **John Locke**, an English political philosopher with his *Two Treatises of Government* and a French Enlightenment thinker, **Jean-Jacques Rousseau** with his *Social Contract*. Americans brought it into practice and thus this theory of politics has been accepted and become central to the Western political tradition.

At first, the colonial forces suffered many defeats because the British army was better equipped and trained. What's more, there was no strong central government to raise money to supply the American army. However, the colonial forces began to win important battles from the end of 1776, under the leadership of George Washington and with the support of most colonists. Encouraged by the colonial victory, the French and Spanish governments gave loans and military support to the colonies in revenge for their past defeats in wars with Britain. A victory at Saratoga in October, 1777 was the turning point of the war and led to an alliance with France. On October 19, 1781, the colonial army won a decisive victory at Yorktown, the British soldiers had to surrender and Britain was forced to the negotiation table. *The Treaty of Paris* was signed in 1783 in which Britain recognized the independence of the 13 colonies.

The Declaration announced the colonists' belief that all people were equal and had some rights that could not be violated such as life, liberty and the pursuit of happiness. The document establishes a principle: if a government violates people's rights, people can overthrow it to preserve their rights and establish a new one to serve them well. The American Revolution gave birth to the first modern republic in the world. It is the first time that colonies defeated tyrannical oppressors and won independence. It sets a good example for other colonies to win independence from their oppressors.

The American Independence War was bourgeois in nature but it did not solve the problem of land demanded by the laboring who had to afford the heavy costs of the war. Dissatisfaction led to uprising in 1786. It came as a terror to the capitalists and the plantation owners. There was a need to build a strong government to protect their life and property. In light of the spirit of *The Declaration of Independence* and the need for a strong government, the Constitutional Convention was held in Philadelphia in May 1787. Delegates were divided and had disputes over the Constitution. Wise and patriotic leaders like George Washington, Benjamin Franklin, Tomas Jefferson, found ways to meet difficult problems. After 4 months of hard work, the Convention

Surrender *v.* 投降
Overthrow *vt.* 推翻
Oppressor *n.* 压迫者
Patriotic *a.* 爱国的
Tip24　为什么说美
国独立战争及其建国
是一场革命?

was finished. James Madison did much to the drafting and was was known as the "Father of the Constitution". It was ratified in 1789 and George Washington was elected the first President. In 1791, the first ten amendments, or the Bill of Rights, were added to the Constitution, guaranteeing the freedom and basic rights of citizens.

Amendment *n.* 修正案
Migration *n.* 迁徙、移民
Crave for 渴求
Sparsely *adv.* 零散稀疏地
Arduous *a.* 艰苦的
Emigrant *n.* 外来移民

IV. Westward Movement

The Westward Movement refers to the continuous migration to the expanded territory of the U.S. and its development by the American people. The process was called the Westward Movement because the new territory was mostly west of the original thirteen colonies.

The land to the west of the Mississippi River used to be France's colony Louisiana. During the French Revolution, it was sold to the United States in 1803. When Mexico became independent in 1921, it had vast territory including Texas, California, Oregon, Arizona, New Mexico. The United States craved for the land and dreamed to expand to the western coast. As more and more Americans immigrated to the sparsely-populated Texas, they announced independence from Mexico and gave the United States good excuse to help Texas against Mexico. The victory in the America-Mexico War (1846-1848) put the U.S. in advantageous condition and Mexico had to concede the vast land which was equal to the whole territory of the United States before the war.

People went West for economic, religious or cultural reasons. The West symbolized cheap or free land or opportunities for economic betterment or the realization of other forms of "American Dream". The trip to the West was long, arduous and sometimes dangerous before modern means of transportation were available, but more and more emigrants moved West, especially during the Gold Rush period. By 1860, about 4.3 million Americans had moved West of the Mississippi. Pioneers may have rosy dreams about life in the West, but they had to start anew in the wild and harsh

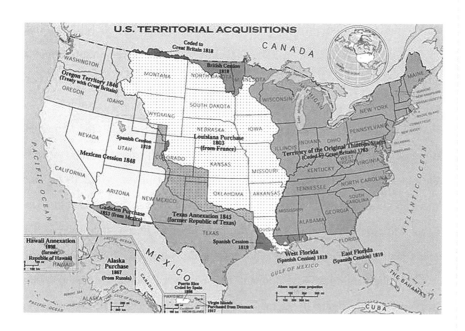

West. Actually only a small fraction of the hopeful emigrants realized their dreams of success. Yet after decades of efforts by generations of migrants, the West was turned into an important center for food production as well as centers of mining and animal husbandry.

Husbandry *n.* 畜牧业
Prosperity *n.* 繁荣
Swarm *v.* 蜂拥

Politically, through the Westward Movement, the U.S. greatly expanded its territorial size and increased its population, two important factors contributing to its rise as a global power. Without the the Westward Movement, the U.S.would be just a medium-sized country limited to the east of the Mississippi River. Nor would it be possible for the U.S. to become a superpower eventually.

Economically, the Westward Movement produced enormous wealth and contributed greatly to the economic prosperity of the U.S. Pioneers cultivated millions of acres of land and made the West an important food production centre. Enough food was produced to feed the ever-growing population and the surplus food was exported to finance the American growth. The West provided rich resources, cheap labor and a huge market for industrial products. The Westward Movement promoted the industrialization. As more people swarmed to the West, businessmen saw a huge profitable market for building highways, canals and railroads and made huge investment which greatly stimulated the growth of transportation. In 1890, U.S. had about 178,000 miles of railroad (280,000 km) with several transcontinental railroads connecting the Atlantic and the Pacific. Hundreds of cities and more towns in the West sprung up and thrived. Chicago is a typical example.

Culturally, the Westward Movement greatly influenced the American national character. The vast West seemed boundless when restless pioneers were not satisfied with the life in one place, they moved to another place. American believe there is always a place for them to realize their dreams. Life in the wilderness required settlers to be independent on themselves. The settlers had to be hard-working and optimistic, otherwise they could hardly survive in the harsh new environment. The Westward Movement has also been a very important source of literary creation, TV series and film productions (Western Movies).

During the process, many Indians were killed or expelled from the land where their ancestors had lived for thousands of years. Many Indian tribes died out and those who survived were driven to Indian reservations. Many historians regard it as one of the most disgraceful stains in American history.

V. American Civil War

American slavery existed since the European immigrants founded their settlements. Many African slaves were employed in the south where the plantations demanded labor resources. During the American Independence War, many slaves fought for the independence. Although the Declaration claimed that all men are created equal, the Negroes are not included. They were regarded as the private property and could be bought or sold.

The fast-growing capitalism, mainly in the free northern states, demanded a unified domestic market, high protective tariffs and free labor, while the southern plantation economy based on slavery prevented the development of capitalism. When Abraham Lincoln won the 1,860 presidential election, South Carolina took the lead in breaking away from the

Thrive v. 繁盛、兴旺
Optimistic a. 乐观的
Expel vt. 驱逐
Ancestor n. 祖先
Disgraceful a. 不体面的
Tariff n. 关税

Union and was followed by six other southern states. They founded the Confederacy of the States of America in 1861, a month before Lincoln swore in.

At that time, Lincoln's first priority was to keep the U.S. as one country; freedom of the slavery was a second objective. After taking office, Lincoln tried hard to preserve the Union by trying to reconcile with the South. The South ignored his efforts and attacked the federal troops in South Carolina. The war with the largest casualties in North America started. To win support from the slaves and the final victory, on January 1, 1863, he issued *The Emancipation Proclamation* which granted freedom to all slaves. The turning point came at Gettysburg in July 1863 — the Union Army defeated the Confederation army. The South surrendered after losing its capital — Richmond — in April, 1865. The North won the war, defended its territorial and sovereignty integrity, and abolished slavery, paving the way for its capitalism and future rise.

The American Civil War is the unfinished part of the American Revolution, a campaign for equality and liberty. Slavery was a shame to many Americans and an irony to the American ideals of equality, liberties and

Reconcile v. 妥协
Casualty n. 伤亡
Sovereignty n. 主权
Integrity n. 完整、正直
Tip25 为什么说美国内战是美国革命的继续? 其意义是什么?

human rights. The American Civil War put an end to slavery and finally brought freedom to all Americans (at least in name), completing the American Revolution. It safeguarded it territorial and sovereignty integrity, removed the obstacles to the development of capitalism in the U.S. and laid a good foundation for the rise of the U.S. as a world power in the 20th century.

Safeguard *vt.* 保卫
Impetus *n.* 动力

VI. Imperialist America and World War I

The Civil War sped up the process of industrialization in the United States, which, in return, brought about many changes in the nation. Before the end of the 19th century, it had already become a highly developed capitalist country and reached the stage of imperialism. Machinery largely replaced the use of hand labor in manufacturing. Transportation and communications were developed to meet the needs of an industrial society: railways and roads connected the east with the west; radios and telegraphs came into daily use. Automobile and ships gave impetus to the growth of oil and steel industries. Big companies replaced small privately owned firms and dominated the economy. By 1894, America had surpassed the U.K. and become the world's leading industrial country. Its total industrial production was almost 7 times than that of 1860, accounting for one third of the world's total.

The great economical strength gave it the power to expand its influence overseas. It looked to Asia and Latin America. In 1880 it occupied the Samoan island and convened the first Pan-American Conference in 1889. To control Cuba, one of the Spanish colonies, it went into war with the Spain in 1898. In the end, Spain was forced to cede the former colonies Cuba, Puerto Rico, Guam and the Philippines to the United States. Moreover, Hawaii was grabbed from the Spain after the war. The Spanish-American War strengthened the U.S. intervention in Latin America. In 1903, after being declined the privilege over Panama, one area of Columbia, the United States cooked a "revolution" in Panama against Columbia and sent troops to prevent the suppressing of the rebellion. After the independence of Panama, a treaty signed granted America the 99 years lease of a canal zone. The Panama Canal was completed in 1914 and shorten the voyage from the Atlantic to the Pacific and greatly promoted the trade.

In the Far East, the United States joined other powers and gained the privilege of consular jurisdiction in China. As it came late, it advocated an **"Open Door Policy"** in 1899, in an attempt to seek equal privileges along with other foreign powers and to guarantee its trade access.

After a decade of expansion, the U.S. became a world power. Yet the world leadership was still in the hands of European powers. The U.S. had to wait before it could exert influence globally. The outbreak of WWI provided America with a chance.

Before WWI, the United States mainly focused on the area of America. To prevent the European from interfering and to dominate the affairs concerning the Latin America, in a State of the Union Address to the congress in 1823, the fifth American President James Monroe declared that the European should not meddle with the American affairs as the United States would not interfere with the European affairs. This is called **Monroe Doctrine**. The United States regarded the Latin America as the backyard. The policy reveals the United States' ambition to dominate and control the whole Latin America.

The outbreak of World War I in 1914 was an inevitable explosion of

Grab *vt.* 攫取
Lease *n.* 租借
Consular jurisdiction 领事管辖权
Interfere *v.* 干涉
State of the Union Address 国情咨文
Meddle *v.* 干涉
Backyard *n.* 后院
Inevitable *a.* 不可避免的
Tip26　从西进运动、美洲政策和亚洲举措,分析19世纪美国对外政策的特点。

Contradiction *n.* 矛盾、
冲突
Neutral *a.* 中立的
Submarine *n.* 潜艇
Treaty *n.* 条约
Extravagant *a.* 奢侈的
Materialism *n.* 物质
主义
Speculation *n.* 投机

contradictions among major powers in the world. It broke out because of fierce rivalry among European powers for raw material and markets in colonies. Following *Monroe Doctrine*, the United States remained neutral in the first few years of the war. During the period, it made huge profits by selling weapons and other supplies to countries involving in the war. It did not enter the war until April 1917 when it decided that the Germans threatened American interests as German submarines tried to sink American ships. Its troop were sent to the Europe when **the Central** and **the Allied** had been greatly weakened in the conflict. The entry of the United States into the war quickened the Germany's defeat.

In an attempt to expand its influence as a world power not only in economy but in world politics, American President Woodrow Wilson proposed a ***Fourteen Points*** program in the negotiation of peace treaty. In his *Fourteen Points*, he defined a new world order of justice, peace and prosperity, promoting freedom of seas, removal of international trade barriers and establishment of the League of Nations as international disputes settler. It was in essence an effort to establish the U.S. domination in the world. However, his ambition was boycotted not only by traditional powers Britain and France but by American congress. The U.S. Senate refused to ratify the Treaty of Versailles. Anyway, with the rise of its economic strength, the U.S. began to play a more and more important role in world affairs.

VII. America in World War II

After World War I, America experienced a period of fast development in the 1920s, which was called the Roaring Twenties. There was an industrial boom. Cars and radios found wide access to more families. People were confident and optimistic about the future. They enjoyed extravagant life and materialism was dominant. Speculation in stocks and bonds, in real estate were popular. All these were reflected in *Great Gatsby*. But it didn't last long. The Great Depression broke out when the New York stock market crashed in October 1929. The financial crisis soon spread to the world and badly affected the economy on the whole. Banks went bankrupt, plants and factory closed, and many people were out of work. People had less capacity to consume, which led to surplus supply and low sales. By 1933, industrial production had fallen to just 56% of 1929 level and at least 13 million people were unemployed.

Bankrupt *a.* 破产的
Diplomatic *a.* 外交的
Remedial *a.* 补救的
Sit-on-the-fence 骑墙
Air raid 空袭

Franklin Roosevelt was elected President in 1933. To deal with the economic depression, he introduced the **New Deal**. Internally, through a huge increase in government expenditure, large scale of public works were undertaken to create employment; externally, efforts were made to consolidate the old markets abroad and conquer new ones. Good Neighbor Policy was adopted toward Latin America and the Untied States even established diplomatic relations with the Soviet Union. The New Deal program had some initial remedial effect but could not solve the crisis completely until a change brought about by the outbreak of World War II.

At the beginning of the war, the U.S. government remained neutral and adopted a sit-on-the-fence policy. The American capitalists wanted to continue their profitable trade with both sides involving in the war. America's attitude began to change in 1940 when in Europe the British were driven out and suffered from repeated air raids and Japan announced its " New Order" to extend its control to the Pacific. The American government began to fear that the Axis countries were winning the war and that their victory would threaten America's security and interest. The Japanese attack on Pearl Harbor brought the United States directly into the war.

To forge a coalition against the fascists, the United States, Britain and China had a conference in Cairo in November 1943, in which leaders from the three countries discussed military issues and arrangement after the war. In June 1944, America, British and Canadian forces landed on the beaches of Normandy, opening the long-delayed western front to attack the Germans when the Soviet Union was fighting against the Germans in the eastern front. In May 1945, Germany surrendered. The Soviet Union sent troops into Northeast China to attack the Japanese. To speed up the collapse of Japan, American airplanes dropped two atomic bombs on Hiroshima and Nagasaki respectively on August 6 and 9. Japan surrendered on August 14 and World War II ended.

Since it entered the war, the United States played an important role in supplying antifascist countries with amount of ammunition and other resources. However, the nature of U.S. imperialism made itself felt. The American monopolists had no scruples in selling arms and other resources to the aggressors. America took over some colonies, occupied many places and turned some, such as Hawaii, into its land or dispatched army there. During the war, the America's economy reached a higher stage and America became the strongest power in the world.

In April 1945, a conference was held in San Francisco to found the United Nations. Fifty-one countries attended, and the headquarters of UN was seated in New York City since then.

VIII. America after World War II

In the early post-war period, **Cold War** was the most important political and diplomatic issue. In the Spring of 1947, American President declared the "Truman Doctrine" which promised economic and military aid to any nation

---

Forge *vt.* 打造

Coalition *n.* 联合、联盟

Collapse *n.* 崩塌、垮塌

Ammunition *n.* 军火

Scruple *n.* 顾虑、顾忌

Tip27　分析美国在两次世界大战期间政策的异同，理解其是如何从一个经济大国逐步成为具有全面影响力的超级大国，这对中国实现民族复兴有何启发？

threatened by an outside power. This marked the beginning of the Cold War. As for the reconstruction in Europe, America came up with the **Marshall Plan** which offered economic aids and loans to help Western European counties to recover. In April 1949, the U.S. allied with other Western countries to form the North Atlantic Treaty Organization (**NATO**).

The Cold War grew out of disagreement in ideology and political system between the Soviet Union and the United States. Each wanted to expand its sphere of influence and restrict the other. Such political, economic and military measures taken by the United States helped the Western Europe to recover from the war and was beneficial to compete with the Soviet Union. Meanwhile another effect was to establish the U.S. hegemony after the war. Thus it led to the conflicts between the two camps of the superpowers.

In 1947, a program was made to investigate the loyalty of federal employees. Later, McCarthy, a Senator proposed a bill in 1950 demanding full investigation and harsh prosecution of communists. While taking the **Containment Policy** to prevent communist ideology from gaining influence in Europe, the U.S. also respond to the challenge in Asia and elsewhere. The Vietnam War (1954-1975) was started under Eisenhower just after the Korean War (1950-1953) and proceeded through the period of John F. Kennedy and Lyndon B. Johnson. In 1960, Kennedy was elected President and his government policy was to contain communism in Vietnam. The Cuba Missile Crisis in 1962 nearly put the world at the brink of nuclear war. In 1963, after President Kennedy was assassinated, Johnson succeeded the office. More and more soldiers were sent to Vietnam. The large-scale and long years war was costly and resulted in large casualty. The war weakened America and sharpened the country's internal contradictions. Many Americans joined demonstrations to oppose the war. Critics rose across the country to demand withdrawal. The election year of 1968 saw the victory of Richard Nixon as President. In terms of diplomacy, Nixon achieved two breakthroughs. His government contacted and reestablished relations with the People's Republic of China; America managed to negotiate with the Soviet Union and signed the first *Strategic Arms Limitation Treaty*. At the beginning

Hegemony *n.* 霸权
Containment policy 遏制政策
Missile *n.* 导弹
Brink *n.* 边缘
Assassinate *vt.* 暗杀
Withdrawal *n.* 撤退/出
Diplomacy *n.* 外交

of his second term, he signed an agreement to bring an end to the Vietnam War in 1973, but he had to resign from office in 1974 because of the Watergate Scandal.

Resign *v.* 辞职
Bloc *n.* 集团
Hostage *n.* 人质
Embassy *n.* 大使馆
Boost *vt.* 刺激
Eliminate *vt.* 清除
Conducive *a.* 有利于的

The competition between the two blocs was intense and full-sized, not only in ideology and politics but also in diplomacy and science. The launch of satellite into the space by the Soviet Union stimulated America to advance its research. During the period, computer was invented. On July 20th, 1969, American astronaut Neil Armstrong became the first human to set foot on the moon.

Jimmy Carter's presidency (1977-1980) experienced an eventful period. The Arab-Israeli war led to the oil crisis and gave impetus to the rising of oil price. To curb the inflation and secure the American dollar's role, oil's price is measured in terms of dollar since 1977. Carter's government decided to established formal relationship with P.R.C. in 1979. The high inflation and his failure in dealing with the hostage crisis of American Embassy in Teheran, Iran brought Carter down in 1980.

Soon after taking office, Ronald Reagan presented a wide-range program in which he called for reductions in income taxes and business taxes in order to boost investment and employment, and proposed deep cuts in federal expenditure covering every area except defense. According to his reform, many government regulations should be eliminated to reduce the federal government's role in business operation. This was called the *laisse-faire* policy in economy and conducive to the business.

With the tight money policy, inflation was finally brought under control and by 1983, a economical recovery was underway. Although many Americans were better off financially than before, Reagan's policy led to an increasing gap between the rich and the poor. Cuts in expenditure drastically reduced the social welfare. Despite these, he won his second term until 1988. At the end of his administration, America was enjoying its longest recorded period of peacetime prosperity without a recession or depression after World War II.

In his first two years in office, George H. W. Bush followed Reagan's economic policy and concentrated on solving the social and economic problems. One important event during his presidency is the Upheaval in Eastern Europe. From the spring, 1989 to 1992, the socialist countries in the Eastern Europe underwent a series of drastic changes in social and political system. The Soviet Union disintegrated into several independent nations in December, 1991. However, Bush's greatest test came when Iraq invaded Kuwait in August, 1990. His government responded by sending American troops which were joined by troops from allied nations. In several weeks, Iraq's army was driven out of Kuwait. Despite the victory in military, he lost the general election in 1992 for the bad performance in economy.

As one of the youngest Presidents in American history, Bill Clinton was ambitious in several issues. Measures for economic recovery were taken and developments began to take shape during the first term. One major achievement was the approval of the *North American Free Trade Agreement* in 1993, which created one of the largest free trade zone in the world. The agreement eliminated most of the import taxes and called for the free flow of goods, services and investments among the United States, Canada and Mexico. In 1999, the trade negotiation between America and China draw to an end and it paved the way for China's entry into WTO. Bill Clinton's second term also saw vigorous economic growth.

IX. America in 21st Century

On September 11th, 2001, only a few months after George W. Bush took office, the United States suffered the most devastating foreign attack ever against its mainland. Terrorists hijacked airplanes and used them as suicide vehicles to destroy the World Trade Center Towers. Thousands of people were killed and the whole country was plunged into deep grieves. The Bush administration took swift and decisive actions. It was declared the country was in a state of war and the American government vowed to bring every criminal to justice. The United States then launched a war against terrorists hidden in

Upheaval *n.* 剧变
Disintegrate *v.* 解体
Take shape 成形
Flow *n.* 流动
Terrorist *n.* 恐怖分子
Hijack *vt.* 劫持
Plunge *vt.* 陷入
Bring... to justice
将……绳之以法

Regime *n.* 政权

Authorize *vt.* 认证、批准

Subprime mortgage 次级抵押贷款

Afghanistan where many terrorist camps were based. As a result, the Taliban regime was removed from power. In 2002 State of the Union Address, Bush named an "axis of the evil", among which Iraq seemed to be the most troublesome. Therefore, the United States waged the Second Gulf War against Iraq in 2003 with supports from several allies. The attack and invasion of Iraq was not authorized by the Security Council of UN and ignored the UN Charter.

Wars in Afghanistan and Iraq were drainage of money and the deployment of soldiers there to maintain security and peace also cost a lot. America could not keep the budget in balance. In 2004, the federal deficit accounted for 3.5% of its Gross Domestic Production(GDP). The Subprime Mortgage Crisis in 2008 brought a blow first to its real estate and financial industry, and later its negative influence was spread to other substantial industries. The unemployment rate rose to nearly 10% in 2009 and remained above it for 16 months.

Barrack Obama won the 2008 election and became the first American President. To cope with the financial crisis, his government lowered interest rate and set aside federal fund to support endangered financial institutions.

However these measures incurred criticism that he stood for the interests of the elite with public fund. His medicare reform expanded the coverage and allowed more poor people to enjoy the social welfare. He also ratified the Paris Climate Accord.

Incur *vt.*招致
Elite *n.* 精英

　　The 2008 financial crisis exposed many social problems in America. Many workers did not enjoy the benefits brought by the boom of IT and finance. Immigrants threatened their job opportunities and their culture. A strong sense of nationalism across America helped Donald Trump stand out and won the 2016 general election. To maintain America's position and suppress China's development, Trump government went to trade war with China by imposing high tariffs on Chinese goods and prohibiting hi-tech products like chips to China.

◎ Exercises

I. Choose the best answer to complete each of the following statements.

1. The first successful English colony in North America was founded at _____ in _____.

　　A. Jamestown, Louisiana　　　　B. Boston, Massachusetts

　　C. Jamestown, Virginia　　　　　D. Plymouth, Georgia

2. The Seven Years War occurred between _____.

　　A. the French and the American Indians

　　B. the French and the Spanish

　　C. the French and the British

　　D. the British and the American Indians

3. No taxation without representation was the rallying slogan of _____.

　　A. the settlers of Virginia　　　　B. the people of Pennsylvania

　　C. the colonists in New England　　D. the people of the 13 colonies

4. In May 1775, _____ was held in Philadelphia and began to assume the functions of a provisional government.

　　A. the First Continental Congress　　B. the Second Continental Congress

　　C. the Boston Tea Party　　　　　　D. the Congress of Confederation

5. Abraham Lincoln issued _____ to grant freedom to all slaves.

    A. *The Declaration of Independence*   B. *The Constitution*

    C. *The Emancipation Proclamation*   D. *The Bill of Rights*

6. The policy of the United States was _____ at the beginning of the two World Wars.

    A. neutrality   B. full involvement

    C. partial involvement   D. appeasement

7. President _____ introduced the New Deal to deal with the problems of the Great Depression.

    A. Wilson   B. Truman

    C. Roosevelt   D. Kennedy

8. Vietnam War was a long time suffering for Americans, and it continued throughout the terms of president _____ .

    A. Johnson, Nixon and Ford   B. Truman, Eisenhower and Kennedy

    C. Kennedy, Johnson and Nixon   D. Eisenhower, Kennedy and Johnson

II. Read the following statements and decide whether they are true (T) or false (F).

1. American was named after Amerigo Vespucci, who arrived on the new continent after Columbus._____

2. The Second Continental Congress was held in Philadelphia, and the Continental Army and Navy was established under the command of Thomas Jefferson._____

3. The American Civil War not only put an end to slavery, but also made American a single, indivisible nation._____

4. Most American people approved of the Vietnam War._____

5. In 1990, American troops and the troops from allied nations took joint military action in order to drive Iraqi troops out of Kuwait._____

6. According to the American government, Saddam Hussein and Osama Bin Laden were responsible for the terrorist event on Septemble11, 2001._____

7. The Bush administration regarded Iraq a nation among the "axis of the evil"._____

8. On March 20, 2003, American and United Nations' troops, supposed by several other countries, began an invasion of Iraq._____

III. Give brief answers to the following questions.

1. How did the U.S.A. develop from 13 colonies into a country across the continent?

2. Why did American change its policy and enter World War Ⅱ?

3. What were Nixon's well-known contributions during his presidency?

4. What were the measure of Reagan's economic program?

5. How does it evolve from revolutionary nation to an imperialist one?

IV. Explain the following in English.

1. Puritanism

2. Westward Movement

3. Open Door Policy

4. Monroe Doctrine

5. Fourteen Points

6. New Deal

7. Cold War

8. Marshall Plan

9. Containment Policy

Chapter 3   Economy

Think and Explore

What's the dispute over the path of development between Hamilton and Jefferson?

What's the essence of New Deal?

What factors contribute to the rising of the U.S.A. as the largest economy in the world?

Why does the U.S.A. turn to neoliberalism in economical policy?

Overview

The U.S. economy is a highly developed free-market economy. The United States is currently the largest and most developed economy in the world, with a diverse economic structure and the U.S. businesses that are global leaders in technology development and innovation.

The economic history of the United States began with the British colonies established in North America between the 17th and 18th centuries. Under the influence of mercantilism, the North American colonies developed a subsistence agricultural economy. Farmers also engaged in handicraft production, and most of the products were used for home consumption. The largest non-agricultural sector was shipbuilding, which accounted for 5% to 20% of total employment.

After the American War of Independence, as an emerging nation, the U.S. economy was still mainly agricultural, with a sparse urban population and reliance on imports for most consumer goods. The year 1787 saw the

Mercantilism *n.* 重商主义

124

Philadelphia Convention, which made the entire country a unified market and gave the federal government the power to tax and mint money.

The year 1790 saw Samuel Slater successfully build the first water-powered spinning mill in the U.S., marking the beginning of American industrialization. In 1793, Eli Whitney invented the cotton gin, which greatly improved the efficiency of cotton picking and promoted the large-scale cultivation of cotton. In 1813, Francis Cabot Lowell established the first integrated cotton spinning and weaving facility, and the U.S. textile industry began to develop, and became the leading industry of the U.S. manufacturing in the early 19th century, and textiles became the main commodity of the U.S. exports. In the 1850s, New England was the first region to industrialize, led by the textile industry. Industrial progress in the North is credited with ensuring Northern victory in the Civil War.

Spinning mill 纺织厂
Cotton gin 轧棉机
Textile *n.* 纺织
Freight *n.* 货物
Gilded Age 镀金时代

Replica of Eli Whitney's 1793 Cotton Gin.

The Bettmann Archive

The widespread use of railroad transportation in the mid-1800s dramatically reduced the cost of freight and passenger transportation. In the late 19th century, the United States entered the "Gilded Age" of rapid economic growth, with the machinery manufacturing industry, separated from the textile industry, becoming the dominant industry. In 1895, the United States surpassed Great Britain in terms of total industrial output and ranked first in the world.

In the 1920s, the rapid growth of the automobile industry and the spread of electricity brought prosperity to the U.S. economy, and welfare capitalism flourished, leading to a significant improvement in the quality of life of the population. After President Franklin D. Roosevelt took office in 1933, the U.S. economy began to recover steadily through new policies that strengthened state intervention in the areas of finance, industry, agriculture, and social security.

The period from the end of World War II to the early 1970s was another golden period of economic growth in the United States. Due to the collapse of *The Bretton Woods Agreement* and the impact of the first oil crisis, the U.S. economy slowed down significantly. In 1981, U.S. President Ronald Reagan implemented Reaganomics, which was based on the economic policy of increasing debt and reducing taxes, increasing the use of neoliberal economic policies and relatively reducing government intervention in the economy.

In the 1990s, the new economic theory brought about by the Internet boom was particularly prevalent, and the speculative capital eventually led to the bursting of the Internet bubble in the early 2000s and the bankruptcy and

Flourish *v.* 兴盛
Neoliberal *a.* 新自由主义的
Speculative *a.* 投机的
Internet Bubble 互联网泡沫

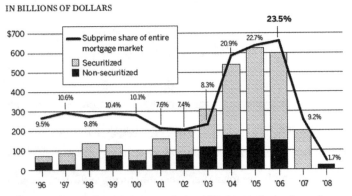

Subprime Mortgage Originations

In 2006, $600 billion of subprime loans were originated, most of which were securitized. That year, subprime lending accounted for 23.5% of all mortgage originations.

IN BILLIONS OF DOLLARS

NOTE: Percent securitized is defined as subprime securities issued divided by originations in a given year. In 2007, securities issued exceeded originations.

SOURCE: Inside Mortgage Finance

liquidation of many Internet communications companies. The year 2007 saw the outbreak of the U.S. subprime mortgage crisis, which in turn triggered a global economic crisis that hit the economy hard, and the 2019 corona-virus pandemic hit the economy hard again.

Trigger *vt.* 触发
Elapse *v.* 流逝
Stagnation *n.* 停滞
Starvation *n.* 饥饿
Salable *a.* 适销的

I. The U.S. Agriculture

One hundred and twenty-six years elapsed from the settlement of Jamestown in 1607 to the settlement of Savannah, Georgia, the thirteenth colony, in 1733. Economic growth was very slow over this long period; but it was not a time of stagnation, and development began to accelerate in the latter part of the period. In the early years, from 1607 to 1640, the incidence of death from starvation, disease, and Indian wars was so high among the settlers that the survival of the settlements was in continuous doubt. By 1640 there were probably no more than 25,000 white people in the English colonies, and by 1700 the settlements still hugged the coasts from Charleston, South Carolina, to what is now Portland, Maine.

The principal concern of most of the settlers during the period 1607 to 1640 was survival itself. Thus, when not engaged in protecting themselves from hostile Indians, the settlers were occupied most of the time with the collection and production of food. The typical settler was a combination of hunter-farmer. The food production ways of the old world were tried in the new unfamiliar environment and usually found wanting; therefore, new ways had to be discovered and tried. These new ways were often learned from the local Indians and were very often concerned with the growing of two crops: Indian corn (or maize) and tobacco. The first crop provided food for survival, the second a salable product which was used to purchase needed supplies. The productivity of the hunter-farmer probably rose from near zero in 1607-1608 to a subsistence level by 1640, and to a level that produced a surplus over subsistence by 1780. From this surplus a few fortunes were made, and the productive capital of agriculture, including black slaves, increased rapidly in the older, settled areas near the coast.

During the American Revolution and the years immediately thereafter, westward expansion and agricultural development were virtually halted. Nonetheless, a trickle of hardy pioneers was moving across the Appalachian Mountains in the 1780s, and by 1790 the trickle had swollen into a stream. This stream had turned into a great westward movement by 1800 — a westward movement of settlers from Georgia to New England. During the nineteenth century, the entire interior of what is now the continental United States was settled. In general terms, this was a 100-year period of extensive growth. Worker productivity in agriculture increased as machines were substituted for human labor. But total output per unit of total input increased very little. This was an age of pioneering, settlement, the adding of resources, and extensive farming.

Agricultural development in the United States changed drastically in the twentieth century. In the first two decades of the century, the rate of increase in agricultural production was slow, but the rate of increase in demand resulting from surging population growth and World War I was rapid, and agriculture enjoyed unparalleled prosperity. A great dynamic process of technological development began to pay off in the 1920s and continued to do so to the present day. Technological developments in the nineteenth century were primarily mechanical, but the emphasis shifted in the twentieth century to include biological and chemical as well as mechanical developments. As a result, agricultural productivity began to increase in the 1930s, and in the 1950s it increased by over 25 percent in one decade. The rate of increase in agricultural productivity slowed slightly in the 1960s and appeared to level off in the early 1970s. Later the rate of increase in agricultural productivity picked up in the second half of the 1970s and raced into the 1980s at an unprecedented pace.

The level of technology and mechanization of the U.S. agriculture is so high that a laborer can grow an average of 1,500 acres, raise 100 cows, feed 5,000 beef cattle and 8,000 pigs. Each farmer can support 128 people. With only 0.3% of the world's labor force, the United States produces 11% of the world's food, 25% of the beef, and 11% of the pork, making it the world's largest exporter of agricultural products. The U.S. Department of Agriculture's Foreign Agricultural Service recently released the 2021 U.S. Agricultural Export Yearbook. The report shows that the total U.S. agricultural exports reached a record $ 177 billion in 2021, with soybean exports reaching $ 27.4 billion, up 7% year-over-year, corn exports reaching $ 18.7 billion, up 103 percent, and beef exports reaching $ 10.6 billion, up 38 percent.

The superior natural resources of the United States provide a strong guarantee for its agricultural development. The plains below 500 meters above sea level in the United States account for 55% of the country's land area, with more than 2.8 billion acres of arable land, accounting for 18.01% of the total land area and 13% of the world's total arable land, and its arable and pasture land account for about 10% of the world's agricultural land. Moreover, more than 70% of the arable land in the United States is concentrated in the Great Plains and inland areas in the form of large contiguous areas with high organic matter in the soil, which is particularly suitable for crop growth. The unique geographical environment and rich land resources provide the necessary material basis for the United States to become the most developed country in the world in terms of agriculture.

Pasture *n.* 牧场
Contiguous *a.* 连续的
Mainstay *n.* 支柱、主要部分
Cereal *n.* 谷物

The mainstay of the U.S. agriculture is the family farm. As of 2017, the total number of family farms in the U.S. is about 2.05 million, and these farms cultivate about 81% of the total farmland in the U.S., provide about 83% of the cereal-based agricultural products in the U.S., and their sales account for about 77% of the agricultural sales in the U.S. On average, each family farm cultivates up to 2,700 acres of land. In terms of the number of people working in agriculture, 5.2 million people are engaged in agricultural production in the United States, making up just 1.3% of the employed the U.S. population, with 25% of farmers with college degrees or higher and only 7% of farmers with less than a high school degree.

However, the U.S. agriculture is also in a major state of transformation. Extreme weather events caused by climate change and the loss of farmland threaten food supplies, and the number of farmers has been slowly declining for decades. At the same time, the tariff war has raised questions about the

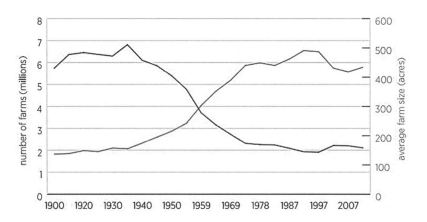

Note: After 1997, the USDA adjusted the figures for coverage.
Source: USDA Census of Agriculture.

financial viability of major crops such as soybeans, the largest food export in the United States. But agriculture is also experiencing rapid innovation. Smart technologies have not only changed the farm labor, but also the way Americans interact with food every day.

II. The U.S. Industry

The United States is the most industrialized country in the world, and industry has traditionally been an important pillar of the U.S. economy. Most of the U.S. industries such as steel, machinery, automobiles, chemicals and other traditional industries are concentrated in the Northeast. In particular, with its developed military industry, warplanes, large warships and aircraft carriers can be produced independently. The main industrial products of the United States are: automobiles, aviation equipment, computers, electronic and communication equipment, steel, petroleum products, fertilizers, cement, plastics and newsprint, machinery, etc.

Among the top ten technology companies in the world, the United States occupies eight. For example, the world-renowned Intel has been providing chips for the world, and especially Microsoft and Oracle occupy the basic market of the software industry.

Pillar *n.* 支柱
Aviation *n.* 航空
Fertilizer *n.* 化肥

The United States has the world's top laboratories, especially in the field of military industry, aerospace, medical technology, information science, etc., the United States is almost unmatched strength and overwhelming scientific and technological advantages of the world's top.

The United States is the world's number one scientific and technological power, especially in the history of human industry has very many of the most important inventions, such as industrial production lines, cotton gin, universal parts, etc., are from the United States, it is worth mentioning that the industrial production lines can be said to be crucial to the development of modern industry, with outstanding and important contributions.

The invention of the production line in the United States took global industrial mass production from a dream to a reality. At the beginning of the 20th century, for example, the automobile was the most fashionable means of transportation at the time, and competition in the automobile industry was fierce. In order to win the competition, the world's major automobile manufacturers were thinking hard to reduce production costs and earn more profits. In 1913, Ford invented the world's first automobile assembly line and started mass production of automobiles. After Ford adopted the assembly line, the efficiency increased greatly, and the time to assemble a car was reduced by more than half. Thanks to the assembly line method, by 1920, Ford's wish of producing one car every minute was completely realized.

There are many other important American technological inventions that can make a long list like cell phone, electric light, telephone, telegraph, phonograph, television, generator, airplane, washing machine, air conditioner, automobile, razor, movie, steam engine, radar, jukebox, color film, cortisone, nylon, toothbrush, napalm, microwave oven, contact lens, credit card, to name a few.

It is worth mentioning that the United States planned three famous projects in the 20th century, such as the Manhattan Project, the Apollo Moon Landing Project and the Human Genome Project. Especially during World War II, the United States was the first to develop the atomic bomb, bringing

Unmatched *a.* 无与伦比的
Mass production 规模化生产
Assembly line 装配线、流水线

technology into the atomic age. At the beginning of the Cold War, the U.S. achieved great success in the field of space technology and led the world in the space race, thus promoting major technological advances in the fields of rocket technology, weapons technology, materials science and computer technology, etc.

In terms of scientific research, a large number of Nobel Prizes have been awarded to the U.S. experts and scholars, especially in the fields of biology and medicine. For example, the National Center for Health Research is an important focus of the U.S. biomedical science, and it has completed the Human Genome Project, allowing humans to enter an important stage in research on cures for tumors, Alzheimer's disease and other diseases. The U.S. National Academy of Sciences, the U.S. National Academy of Engineering, the U.S. National Academy of Medicine and the U.S. National Endowment for Nature are the four major academic institutions at the highest level of the U.S. science.

The U.S. economy is dominated by high-end manufacturing and high-tech industries, including aerospace, aircraft manufacturing, automobile manufacturing, computers, chemicals, machinery, biotechnology, microelectronics, new materials, pharmaceuticals, semiconductors, and many other industrial sectors, and ranks as a world leader. The United States produces many industrial giants: such as the world-renowned Boeing, General Electric, Intel, General Motors, Exxon Mobil, Chevron, Ford, etc.

The U.S. industry is very uneven in regional distribution, mainly concentrated from the Mississippi River in the west, east to the Atlantic coast, the Ohio River and Potomac River from the south, to the south of Lake Michigan, Lake Erie and Lake Ontario shore in the north, and the southern part of New England. This dense eastwest narrow strip of industry, is known as the United States "manufacturing belt". Its area only accounts for about 8% of the country, but it concentrates more than 1/2 of the manufacturing industry in the United States, becoming the most concentrated area of industry in the country. During the Second World War and after, in the Western Pacific coast of California and other states, some military-related emerging

Cure *n.* 疗法、药物
Tumor *n.* 肿瘤

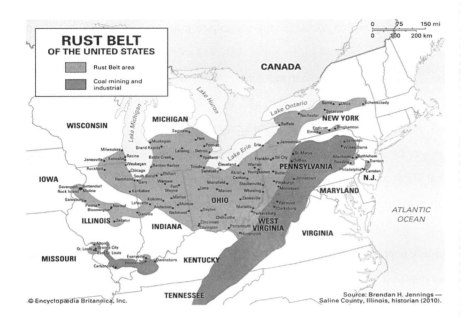

industrial sectors, such as shipbuilding, aircraft, missiles, electronics, automotive assembly, etc., have been developed tremendously. Since the 1970s, the economy and population have shifted southward. The industrial development in the south and west, known as the "Sunbelt," has been faster than that in the northeast.

III. The U.S. Service Industry

With the accelerated process of economic globalization, increased international market space, upgraded industrial structure and increasingly refined international division of labor, the service industry has become independent and one of the leading industries in the world today. The United States is undoubtedly a superpower in the service industry today, which includes wholesale, retail, transportation, warehousing, information industry, finance, insurance, real estate, leasing, professional and business services, education, medical care, social assistance, entertainment, accommodation and catering, government and other services.

The U.S. service industry started early and has gone through roughly two stages of development. The first stage was from the early 19th century to the 1950s, during which the U.S. service industry developed steadily, with the service industry accounting for more than 50% of GDP and more than 50% of total employment. In the second phase, from the 1950s to the present, the U.S. service sector grew rapidly, and while the share of the U.S. agricultural and industrial output declined significantly from 1960 to 2010, the share of the service sector in the U.S. GDP continued to rise, accounting for 58% of total GDP and 62.3% of total employment from 1960. By 2010, its GDP accounted for 80% of total GDP and its employment accounted for 90% of total employment. With a 14% increase in its total GDP and a 40% increase in employment, the dominance of the U.S. services sector in national economic development has become more apparent.

Since 1971, the U.S. trade has basically been in deficit due to the long-standing deficit in goods trade, which accounts for a large share of the U.S. trade. From 1980 onwards, trade in services developed rapidly, greatly filling the huge deficit in goods trade and accounting for an ever-increasing proportion. The total import and export of trade in services rapidly expanded from $102.9 billion in 1981 to $951.9 billion in 2010, an increase of more than 9 times, much faster than the development of the U.S. goods trade. The U.S. services trade has obvious advantages in the world. In 2010, the total import and export of world services trade was $716.6 billion, of which the U.S. accounted for 13.28%, which is incomparable to any other countries. The development of the U.S. service industry not only provides a strong impetus to the development of the national economy, but also plays a role in stabilizing the balanced development of the national economy.

Since 1960, the value added of the service sector in the U.S. has been rising as a share of total GDP, increasing by nearly 30 percentage points. By 2010, the service sector provided jobs for more than 90% of Americans, making it the number one industry in the U.S. and playing an increasingly significant role in its economic development, foreign trade, and especially in increasing employment.

The value added of all sectors of the service industry has been increasing, and the share of GDP and employment in most sectors has been steadily rising. Although the share of value added of a few industrial sectors has declined, the value created by them as a whole has continued to increase in line with the U.S. economic development. The distribution of employment in each industry is also becoming more reasonable, and most industries maintain an absolute lead in the world and are highly competitive.

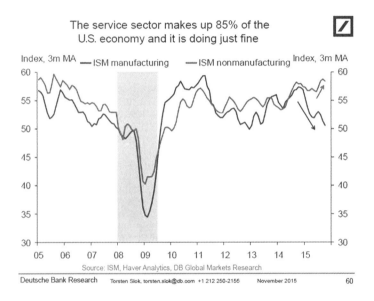

The service sector makes up 85% of the U.S. economy and it is doing just fine

Source: ISM, Haver Analytics, DB Global Markets Research

Deutsche Bank Research   Torsten Slok, torsten.slok@db.com +1 212 250-2155   November 2015   60

The proportion of traditional service industry to the value added of service industry is decreasing, and the proportion of modern service industry to the value added of service industry is increasing very conspicuously. The proportion of traditional service industries in the service industry, represented by wholesale and retail, transportation, entertainment, catering, etc., has been decreasing year by year, and the rate of decrease is obvious. The ratio of the added value of these service industries to GDP dropped from 41.7% in 1960 to 22.3% in 2010, decreasing by nearly half, and the employment rate also dropped. On the other hand, modern service industries, represented by information, finance and business services, have been rising rapidly, and the value added to GDP ratio has been increasing from 31.1% in 1960 to 47.2% in 2010. The modern service industry occupies a major position in the national

Wholesale *n.* 批发
Retail *n.* 零售
Catering *n.* 餐饮

economy, driving the development of the U.S. economy, and will play an increasingly important role in economy.

The value added of public welfare services, mainly education, medical care and social assistance, has increased significantly as a share of GDP, from 2.7% in 1960 to 8.7% in 2010, and has increasingly become a major industry in the U.S. service industry sector. The U.S. government's investment in these industries is also increasing.

The evolution of the U.S. services policy has also been divided into two main phases. The first stage was from the 1930s to the 1960s, when the U.S. government intervened and regulated the service industry more than any other time. Specific policy measures were mainly to increase government investment, strengthen infrastructure construction, establish and improve the social security system, encourage the development of high-tech industries, open up markets and create opportunities for new products and industries. Meanwhile, the financial service industry was strictly regulated. In the second phase, from the 1970s to the present, the U.S. government's service industry policy has been characterized by deregulation and opening to the outside world, encouraging innovation and focusing on efficiency, promoting competition and stimulating the vitality of the service industry.

Deregulation *n.* 放松管制
Vitality *n.* 活力
Spark *vt.* 激发
Fiscal *a.* 财政的
Partisan *a.* 党派的

IV. American Economic Policies

It is generally believed that the 100-year period from the early 19th century to the early 20th century was the period when the United States completed its transformation from an agricultural country to an industrial country, and then became an industrial and agricultural power.

However, when the republic was first founded, Alexander Hamilton, the first Secretary of the Treasury, and Thomas Jefferson, the Secretary of State, was engaged in a heated debate over the general policy of the government. The debate between Hamilton and Jefferson was sparked by fiscal and economic policies, and then expanded to include the Constitution, the political system, and foreign policies. The debate was not a general policy disagreement, nor was it merely a personal and partisan dispute, but a major issue concerning the path of development after the founding of the United States. The two Founding Fathers actually proposed two different paths to nationhood, with Hamilton focusing on the world trend and advocating the path of industry and commerce while Jefferson emphasized the uniqueness of the United States and advocated the path of agriculture. The two different paths of nation-building formed the focus of their arguments.

A Statue of Alexander Hamilton Stands in Central Park in New York, AP Photo

The reason why Hamilton actively advocated the development of industry and commerce was that he saw the trend of accelerated development of industry and commerce in modern Western Europe including Britain after the beginning of the Industrial Revolution. He analyzed the history of the rise of industry and commerce in Europe, pointing out that since the late Middle Ages, the promotion of commerce and manufacturing has increasingly become the national policy of different countries like Britain, France, the Netherlands, and Spain. Even Russia and Turkey are committed to commerce and manufacturing. He believed that after the founding of the United States, it was necessary to follow this world trend and to quickly achieve the United States' rise as one of the industrial and commercial powers.

Agrarianism *n.* 唯农
论、平均地权论

Decay *n.* 腐朽,腐化

Barometer *n.* 晴雨表

Cannibalistic *a.* 吃
人的

Accommodate *vt.*
为……提供食宿

Prescient *n.* 有先见之
明的人

Tip28   美国建国之
后,杰弗逊和汉密尔
顿争论的实质是什
么?

Unlike Hamilton's path of nation-building, Jefferson was influenced by agrarianism and advocated the establishment of the United States as an agricultural nation after independence, avoiding the path of developing commerce and industry and big cities like those in Western European countries. Jefferson advocated that the new republic should be committed to vigorously developing agriculture, and establishing a democratic republic with free farmers as the mainstay. Jefferson's view was mainly based on the consideration of maintaining social justice and preventing the decay of the republican system of government. In his view, farmers who worked on free land had high and innocent morals, and the proportion of farmers to other citizens in a country was a barometer of the degree of corruption. If the United States was to build manufacturing industries and cities, it would become as corrupt and cannibalistic as the inhabitants of Europe, and the democratic republic would be seriously threatened. He also believes that the rise of manufacturing in Europe is due to overpopulation and limited land, while the vast land in the western United States can accommodate a large number of people, and therefore should not develop manufacturing.

Hamilton can be regarded as the most prescient of the Founding Fathers on predicting the industrial future of the United States. During the 80 years from 1812, when the U.S. manufacturing industry began to develop after the Anglo-American War, to 1894 when its industrial output value leaped to the first place in the world, the U.S. succeeded in achieving a rapid economic rise through a protectionist trade policy, a gradually unified domestic market, abundant natural resources, greatly improved transportation conditions, and rapidly advancing science and technology. The U.S. success story at that time boils down to one thing: it has implemented a long-term domestic demand-led economic development strategy. This is mainly manifested in four aspects: First, from the Civil War to 1914, the U.S. foreign trade dependence has been very low, remaining between 12% and 14.1% for a long time. Second, domestic consumption was the engine of economic growth. In the years before World War I, Britain exported 1/4 of its industrial goods, but the U.S.

exported less than 1/10 of its industrial goods. Third, there was a serious inward bias in business, and the U.S. companies were only interested in foreign markets once they had established a national sales distribution network. Finally, the rise of the U.S. economy was achieved through a "brick wall" of high tariff protection.

The Civil War had a tremendous impact on the U.S. economic development and economic policy. During the Civil War, the federal government raised tariff rates to support the costly war effort. Although much of this practice stemmed from the need to finance the war, protectionist policies were gradually institutionalized as the ideology of protecting and promoting American manufacturing began to dominate both inside and outside the government even after peace was restored, and even though various temporary domestic taxes were quickly eliminated, tariff rates not only did not return to their pre-war levels, but continued to climb higher. The Civil War greatly accelerated the process of industrial development in the U.S. In the 1860s alone, the country saw a 56.6 percent increase in wage and a 79.6 percent increase in the number of factories.

In the eyes of the emerging industrial bourgeoisie and the general public at this time, restrictions on domestic private capital were not only unnecessary but also had serious consequences; capital could only be used to further develop its rich natural resources and make its fruits available to all members of society only if it was helped, not hindered, by the power of the state. Guided by this ideology, the development of manufacturing in the United States gradually produced two results: first, a unique industrial system was formed, and various manufacturing industries began to participate in and eventually lead the second industrial revolution worldwide, and an explosive increase in the level of productivity occurred along with the rapid advancement of science and technology; second, excessive competition also gave rise to the emergence of industrial monopolies. With the evolving trend of corporate mergers, the United States gradually completed the transition from competitive capitalism to monopoly capitalism.

On December 2, 1823, President James Monroe delivered his State of the Union address, setting forth three core principles, the first of which was opposition to the establishment of new colonies in America by European powers, the second of which was opposition to interference by European powers in already independent American countries, and the third of which declared that the United States would not interfere in the affairs of European countries, often referred to as isolationism. Monroe set a basic framework for the U.S. international strategy in the 19th century, but the so-called *Monroe Doctrine* was constantly reinterpreted in the 19th century, evolving from a principle of protecting one's own country or region from outside interference to one of actively seeking regional hegemony. After the Civil War, the United States, by virtue of the Second Industrial Revolution, increased its industrial and military power. The U.S. government's interpretation and application of the *Monroe Doctrine* had increasingly moved in the direction of constructing regional hegemony.

James Monroe

National Portrait Gallery/Smithsonian

At the beginning of the 20th century, the United States was already the largest industrial country in the world, with a large amount of capital surplus, which was bound to be exported to the outside world. A series of Central

American and Caribbean countries have a large amount of debt to European powers, which the U.S. government believes may trigger interference from European powers. For the security of America, it is necessary for the United States to provide loans to these countries to repay the debts of European powers. After turning into a creditor of these countries, the United States tried to control the customs and financial order of these countries, and even subverted their regimes through military intervention to ensure the return on their investment. Countries such as Nicaragua, Haiti, Dominica and Honduras have all learned the terror of American "Dollar Diplomacy". It can be said that in this way the original "Monroe Doctrine" has further developed into a more sophisticated "Economic Monroe Doctrine".

Subvert *vt.* 颠覆
Abandon *vt.* 抛弃
Erupt *v.* 爆发
Allocation *n.* 分配
Exacerbation *n.* 恶化
Expedient *n.* 权宜之计、应急之策

The U.S. government abandoned traditional liberal policies after World War II. The U.S. made extensive social improvements in labor relations, social distribution, and financial regulation, and the fruits of technological progress and productivity gains benefited more of the lower and middle classes, resulting in a golden period of steady economic growth and narrowing of the gap between rich and poor, a rare period in history. The Western media claimed that the institutional and policy innovations of this period originated from Keynesianism, but in fact it was more a case of the United States borrowing from Marxism because of the pressure of the Cold War.

The economic crisis that erupted in the United States in the 1930s and then in the capitalist countries fully exposed the inherent flaws of the capitalist market economy system, which, without state macroeconomic regulation, promoted the efficient allocation of resources, but also exacerbated the deviation of the scale of production from the scale of the market, thus further deepening the degree of recession in the economic cycle. Although the *New Deal* launched by President Franklin D. Roosevelt and the wartime economic policies during World War II were only expedient measures during the special period and did not have a systematic, comprehensive and coherent theoretical basis for state macro-control, they laid the practical foundation for state intervention in the economy from the 1960s.

The economic policy of macro-control in the United States has roughly

President Franklin D. Roosevelt Signed the Social Security Bill on August 14, 1935.

Compensatory *a.* 补偿性的
Expansionary *a.* 扩张性的

gone through several stages. The first stage is the Keynesian period from the end of 1970s after World War II, the Truman administration and the Eisenhower administration implemented compensatory fiscal policy. From the Kennedy administration in the 1960s to the Carter administration in the 1970s, the U.S. began to adopt the Keynesian theory of "Effective Demand" as a theoretical guide and adopted mainly expansionary policies to intervene in the U.S. macro-economy. The second phase was from the Reagan administration in the 1980s. Since Keynesianism could not do anything about the "stagflation" that occurred in the U.S. in the 1970s, neoliberalism emerged at this time. The third stage started with the Clinton administration in the 1990s. Clinton abandoned the one-sided pursuit of demand management or supply management economic policy, and carried out macro-control of the national economy from both the supply and demand sides, and truly achieved inflation-free economic growth. The fourth stage is since the 21st century. Following the global financial crisis triggered by the U.S. subprime mortgage crisis in 2008, the Obama administration launched the macro-control characterized by the use of a huge amount of money and implemented a quantitative easing monetary policy. During the development of the U.S. economy, the two major types of approaches, government intervention in the economy and liberalism, have influenced the formulation of the U.S. economic policies.

Since 2017, the policy orientation and specific practices of the new U.S. administration signify the revival of its economic unilateralism. It has adopted a series of unilateral measures such as trade protectionism, economic sanctions and extreme pressure against many countries in the world, including Latin American countries. Since taking office, the Trump administration, under the banners of "America First" and "Make America Great Again, " has made a series of major adjustments to the U.S. foreign policies, particularly in the economic and trade areas. A series of major adjustments, which is particularly prominent in the field of economic and trade. He not only announced in high profile the withdrawal from the Trans-Pacific Partnership (TPP), a significant reduction in foreign aid, the implementation of high tariffs, the restart of NAFTA negotiations, but also strongly provoked trade friction between China and the United States, and even threatened to withdraw from the World Trade Organization (WTO). Trump has proposed to reduce government regulation, including reducing regulations on businesses and correcting over-regulation of the financial system. Tax cuts and deregulation were important ideas of the supply school in the Reagan era. The Trump administration's economic unilateralism will have a series of far-reaching effects on world economic growth, multilateral international mechanisms, U.S.-China relations, and the international political and economic order as a whole.

Unilateralism *n.* 单边主义
Sanction *n.* 制裁, 禁运
Provoke *vt.* 刺激
Far-reaching *a.* 影响深远的

◎ Exercises

I. Choose the best answer from the four choices.

1. After the American War of Independence, the U.S. economy was still mainly _____ , with a sparse urban population and reliance on imports for most consumer goods.

　A. agricultural　　　　　　B. industrial

　C. cotton　　　　　　　　D. shipbuilding

2. The mainstay of the U.S. agriculture is the _____. As of 2017, the total number of family farms in the U.S. is about 2.05 million, and these farms cultivate about 81% of the total farmland in the U.S.

A. cotton　　　　　　　　B. tobacco

C. pasture land　　　　　　D. family farm

3. During World War II, _____ was the first to develop the atomic bomb, bringing technology into the atomic age.

A. the U.S.S.R.　　　　　　B. the U.S.A.

C. Japan　　　　　　　　　D. China

4. Traditionally, the U.S. industry is very uneven in regional distribution, mainly concentrated in the _____.

A. Sun Belt　　　　　　　B. Black Belt

C. Bible Belt　　　　　　　D. Manufacturing Belt

5. By 2010, the _____ sector provided jobs for more than 90% of Americans, making it the number one industry in the U.S. and playing an increasingly significant role.

A. service　　　　　　　　B. chip

C. real estate　　　　　　　D. medical care

6. When the republic was first founded, the debate between _____ and Jefferson was sparked by fiscal and economic policies, and then expanded to include the Constitution, the political system, and foreign policies.

A. Adams　　　　　　　　B. Madison

C. Hamilton　　　　　　　D. Washington

II. Decide whether the following statements are true (T) or false (F).

1. The period from the end of World War I to the early 1970s was another golden period of economic growth in the United States. _____

2. Agricultural development in the United States did not change much in the twentieth century. _____

3. At the beginning of the Cold War, the U.S. achieved great success in the field of space technology and led the world in the space race. _____

4. Thomas Jefferson was influenced by mercantilism and advocated the establishment of the United States as an industrial nation after independence. _____

III. Give brief answers to the following questions.

1. What are the major changes taking place in American agriculture in the 20th century?

2. What was the focus of the arguments between Alexander Hamilton and Thomas Jefferson?

Chapter 4 Politics

Think and Explore

Why does the U.S.A. adopt Federalism?

How does checks and balances operate?

Compare the political system between the U.S.A. and the U.K.

Why is the running for the American Presidency a kind of money game ?

Overview

Different from U.K., the United States has its written Constitution which is the supreme law and determines the fundamental system of the nation. The Constitution of the United States is based on the Independence Proclamation and formulated in 1787.

Proclamation *n.* 宣言
Formulate *vt.* 制定
Abuse *n.* 滥用
Compromise *n.* 妥协
Preamble *n.* 序 言、前言
Tranquility *n.* 宁静
Ordain *vt.* 规定

During the Constitutional Convention in Philadelphia, 55 delegates from 13 colonies had heated and thorough discussion. Their major concerns focus on three issues: how states would be represented? how to avoid power abuse and protect people's rights and liberty ? how to deal with the slavery issue?

Through negotiation and compromises, they found common grounds over the former two issues and reached the agreement. The Preamble to the Constitution reveals the basis and reasons for forming government:

We the people of the United States, in order to form a more perfect union, establish justice, insure domestic tranquility, provide for the common defense, promote the general welfare, and secure the blessings of liberty to ourselves and our posterity, do ordain and establish this Constitution for the

United States of America.

The U.S. political system was established on the basis of three main principles: federalism, the separation of powers, and the rule of law and respect for the Constitution.

The United States is a federal union of 50 states, with the District of Columbia as the seat of the federal government. America adopts federalism in which individual states unite under a central government and power is divided between national and state governments. The federal government only deals with federal issues. Over state issues, the state government has the final say and the federal government is unable to intervene, vice versa.

To avoid power abuse, they believe that nobody shall enjoy absolute power and power should be separated, and that power should be supervised and checked. Power is divided into three parts which are represented by legal branch, executive branch, and judicial branch respectively. To restrict their power and to achieve a balance in power, each branch can monitor or restrains other two branches and each branch can not ignore or overpower other branches. This is the mechanism of Checks and Balances. For example, the Congress passes bills while the President can approve or veto them conditionally; the Supreme Court reviews the constitutionality of any law or decision of cases; the Congress makes laws, approves the budget and even can impeach the President. The system of checks and balance means the constitutional division of powers among the legislative, executive and judicial branches in order to prevent abuse of power.

Ten amendments were introduced in 1789, which specified individual rights like freedom of speech, religion, press, assembly, the rights of bearing arms, justice of trials, etc. The ten amendments is also called *The Bill of Rights*. Later, other amendments are added including the 13th which abolishes slavery; the14th protects life, liberty, pursuit of happiness; the 15th which grants the right to vote; the 24th which guarantees voting not based on taxes and the 19th which ensures voting rights for women.

Check *vt.* 审查
Restrain *vt.* 限制
Veto *vt.* 否决
Constitutionality *n.* 合宪性
Budget *n.* 预算
Impeach *vt.* 弹劾
Tip29   结合美国宪法,理解并分析三权分立与制衡机制。

I . The Legislature

American Congress is the law-making and supreme legislative branch, consisting of two houses: the Senate and the House of Representatives. The main function of Congress is to make federal laws and decide on the budget. Both houses have the power to introduce legislation on any subject except the revenue bills which must be originate in the House of Representatives.

The Senate had 100 senators, serving a six-year term. Representation in the Senate is based in the principle of state equality: each state, whether it is big or small, has two senators. The Senate enjoys the following exclusive powers: to try impeachment cases, to approve presidential appointments, to ratify treaties and so on. The Vice President chairs the Senate.

The House of Representatives has 435 voting members. Each state receives representation in proportion to its population but is entitled to at least one Representative. The term of Representatives is two years. Every two years, all Representatives shall be elected. Compared with the Senate, the House of Representatives has the exclusive power to introduce tax bills and initiate impeachments. The head of the House comes from the winning party and is called the Speaker.

A member of either house can introduce a bill or legislative proposal which will be sent to a proper committee. The committee or its sub-committee holds a series of sessions to discuss the bill or hear opinions from different stakeholders. After the hearings, the committee will vote on the bill to see if it should proceed further. If it survives, recommendations regarding the bill will be reported to the House or the Senate. If two houses approve similar bills with different opinions, two versions will be submitted to a Conference Committee, which manages to work out a compromise. Otherwise, the bill will die. Once it is passed in both houses, the bill will be called an *Act* and go to the President for approval who may either sign it into law or veto it. If it is vetoed, congress can override the veto by a two-thirds majority and the bill will become a law immediately.

Revenue *n.* 收入
Stakeholder *n.* 利益攸关者
Override *vt.* 推翻、不理会
Tip30　美国参众两院在功能上有何不同?

II. The Executive

The executive is responsible for the administration of the U.S. laws, consisting of 15 departments and many independent agencies. It is headed by the President.

The President of the United States is one of only two nationally elected federal officers, the other being the Vice President of the United States. He is the supreme and symbolic leader of country, and the Commander-in-chief of the U.S. armed forces. He has the power to appoint or nominate important federal officials and ambassadors. Moreover, he is the Chief of State, in charge of the operation of government.

Nominate *vt.* 提名
Hierarchical *a.* 层级的
Complementary *a.* 互补的

The Cabinet is the major source of advice and assistance to the President. It is made up of the heads of the major departments and other persons chosen by the President. Usually it includes the White House Office, the National Security Council, the Council of Economic Advisers and the Office of Management and Budget.

American President enjoys enormous power but his power is not unlimited. He must turn to Congress for every dollar to sustain the operation of federal government. His nomination of officials must be confirmed by the Senate. Finally, he may be impeached by Congress if he abuses his power or commits a crime.

III. The Judiciary

The judicial branch consist of two separate, but contiguous systems: the federal court system and the state court system. They are both hierarchical, and are separated and independent but complementary with each other.

The federal law court is composed of three levels: the Supreme Court, the courts of appeals, and the district courts. The Supreme Court, which is the highest court in the federal system, and the only court created by the U.S. Constitution. There are one chief justice and eight associate justices. They are

Misconduct *n.* 不当/
不法行为
Intermediate *a.* 中级的
Appellate *a.* 上诉的
Jurisdiction *n.* 司法管
辖（权）
Uphold *vt.* 维护（法
律、正义）
Applicable *a.* 适用的
Verdict *n.* （陪审团
的）裁决、裁定

appointed by the President with the consent of the Senate. They serve for life, and can only be removed by impeachment for misconduct, but their powers can be limited by the President and Congress. The major powers of the Supreme Court as follows: a) to interpret laws; b) to hear appeals from any federal court; c) to review cases concerning Constitution or national laws; d) may declare a law or a presidential act unconstitutional. Moreover, all cases concerning ambassadors, ministers and consuls of foreign countries, and cases in which a state is involved, can go directly to the Supreme Court. Decisions are made by the majority.

The courts of appeals are the intermediate appellate courts. Now the whole country is divided into 12 Regional Circuit Courts of Appeal and 1 Court of Appeals for the Federal Circuit. They review decisions of federal district courts. Judges from the Court of Appeals usually do not review facts or take additional evidence. They just examine trial record for mistakes in applying law. Cases are reviewed without jury.

There are 94 federal district courts, including at least one district court in each state. They are the lowest unit of the federal court system and courts of original jurisdiction, where civil and criminal cases begin and are tried. The decision of Courts of Appeal are final except when they are reviewed by the Supreme Court.

Besides the federal judicial system, each state has its own judicial system, the police force and the prison system. Most legal cases take place in the state system. State judges and police forces are responsible for upholding the state law. State judicial systems are not exactly alike, but share the general structure: Trial Courts of General Jurisdiction, Intermediate Appellate Courts and State Supreme Court.

All American courts adopt the jury system and common law in which precedents are binding. After hearing the evidence, the judge explains the applicable law to the jury who shall reach a verdict in secret.

IV. Political Parties

A two-party system is dominant in the United States, and they are the Democratic Party and the Republican Party.

The Democratic Party is historically the party of laborers, minorities and progressive reformers. It opposes unregulated business and finance. The Democrats want the government to play an important role in the economy and emphasize full or high employment. They usually favor civil rights laws, strong social security, income taxes and are supportive of abortion, same-sex marriage, gun control, etc. The symbol of the Democratic Party is a donkey.

The Republican Party, founded in 1854 as an anti-slavery party, came to power in 1860 as its candidate Abraham Lincoln won the election. It represents the interests of big businesses and prosperous farmers of the West. The Republicans favor an economic system which gives enterprises greater freedom and demand that the government control inflation. They stress the need for law and order. They oppose complete government social program, abortion, same-sex marriage, gun control, etc. The symbol of the Republican Party is an elephant.

There are no special requirements for membership of the two parties. There are no membership cards, no dues, no initiation ceremonies. They are not required to attend meetings or pay for party expenses. Party members can change their membership easily or don't vote for party candidates. All are voluntary. That is to say, party membership is nothing but an expression by the voter of which party he prefers.

Since World War II, the two parties have dominated the presidency in turn. Generally speaking, the Democratic Party has a liberal ideology while the Republican Party is more conservative. This affects their attitude towards economic issues, social issues and foreign affairs, etc. The two parities are both bourgeois in nature. Whichever party come into power, the basic policies are similar or the same.

Minorities *n.* 少数群体、少数民族

Abortion *n.* 堕胎、流产、丑陋

Dues *n.* 会费

Tip31　从两党的政治理念与政策实施分析美国两党制的实质。

V. The General Election

The general election is held every 4 years on the first Tuesday in November, called Election Day. The President and the Vice President are elected indirectly by Electoral College process. The general election is to choose presidential electors in their state who make up the Electoral College. The number of presidential electors in each state is equal to that of its senators and representatives in Congress. That is to say, the general election will not only elect the President and the Vice President but also elect the congress at the same time. The total number of presidential electors is currently 538,535 from 50 states and 3 from Washington D.C.

By law, any natural-born American citizen over 35 years old can run for the presidency. However, in reality, only the candidates nominated by the two major parties have the chance to win the presidential election. One reason is that a candidate has to spend a lot of money to gain support across the country. Selecting the right candidate for the presidency is very important for both parties. To do this, each party usually goes through several stages.

1. The Primary Election

All the aspirants for the nomination start their personal campaigns within the party. Their purpose is to have their supporters chosen as delegates to the party's national convention. The more supporters they have, the greater the chance for them to be nominated for the candidacy. This process is called the primacy election.

2. The National Convention

Each party holds its national conventions every four years, usually in the summer before the general election. Though the national convention discusses and decides on the party's general policy for both domestic and foreign affairs, the main job is to choose a presidential candidate. The final choice is made when one candidate has received more than half of the votes. If not, a

Electoral College 选举人团

Aspirant *n.* 有抱负的人

Ballot *n.* 选票, 投票

second or third ballot will be held. After the convention, the whole party will help the candidate run for the election across the country. There will a team to help the candidate to run for the presidency.

The candidate has to travel all over the country, making countless speeches and interacting with local people. They pay visits, attend meetings, make phone calls and take part in TV programs to publicize their policy and to gain support. Each party make posters, produce video, issue advertisements in newspapers and TV. Nowadays, social media become a new battle field to compete. It is a routine that candidates from the two parties will have three public debates on television 3 months before the Election Day. The live debates will be broadcast to the whole nation to give voters opportunities to better understand the candidates and their policies. All the campaign activities consume a lot of resources and money. So one of the main job for the president candidates and their parties' national committees is to raise fund.

The general election can be divided into two stages. For the first stage, presidential electors for each state will be chosen. The candidate with the most votes in a state wins all of that state's electoral votes, known as the "winner-take-all" principle. There are 48 states that follow the winner-takes-all rule. All presidential electors compose the Electoral College. During the second stage, the electors meet and vote to select a President. Since all the electors have pledged to vote for a given candidate, the second stage is actually a formality. Everyone knows who will be the next President when the first stage is finished.

It is reported that the two parties spent almost 7 billions dollars for the campaign in 2016 general election. Somebody says that the American president election is a game for the rich and common people can not afford it.

Publicize *vt.* 宣传
Formality *n.* 礼节、正式手续
Tip32 为什么说美国大选在某种程度上是富人的游戏？

◎ Exercises

I. Choose the best answer to complete each of the following statements.

1. The US. Constitution came into effect in _____.

   A. 1787   B. 1789

C. 1791   D. 1793

2. The Constitution of the United States _____.

   A. gives the most power to Congress

   B. gives the most power to the President

   C. tries to give each branch enough power to balance the others

   D. gives the most power to the Supreme Court

3. *The Bill of Right* _____.

   A. defines the rights of Congress and the rights of the President

   B. guarantees citizens of the U.S. specific individual rights and freedom

   C. is part of the *Declaration of Independence*

   D. has no relationship with the Constitution

4. The terms for a Senator and Representative are _____ and _____ years respectively.

   A. 2; 4   B. 2; 3

   C. 2; 6   D. 6; 2

5. All the followings can make legislative proposals EXCEPT _____.

   A. the senator   B. the representative

   C. the secretary of state   D. the president

6. The followings are all powers of the President EXCEPT _____.

   A. vetoing any bills passed by Congress

   B. appointing federal judges when vacancies occur

   C. making laws

   D. issuing executive orders

7. The Supreme Court is composed of _____ justices.

   A. 6   B. 7

   C. 8   D. 9

8. The president is directly voted into office by _____

   A. all citizens of America   B. the citizens over 18 years old

   C. electors elected by the voters D. the senators and the representatives

II. Read the following statements and decide whether they are true(T) or false (F).

1. *The Bill of Right* was written into the Constitution in 1787. _____

2. The form of the American government is based on three main principles: federalism, the

separation of powers and respect for the Constitution and rule of law. _____

3. The U.S. Congress consists of two houses: the House of Commons and the House of Lords.
   _____

4. The judicial branch of the U.S. federal government consists of a series of courts: the Supreme
   Court, the courts of appeals and the district courts. _____

5. The Democratic Party is conservative in terms of its ideology. _____

6. The American presidential campaigns adhere to the winner-takes-all practice. _____

7. The American foreign policy throughout World War II was neutrality. _____

8. The American foreign policy during the Cold War period was containment and intervention.
   _____

III. Give brief answers to the following questions.

1. What are the two characteristics of the U.S. Constitution?

2. What are the qualifications for a senator and a representative respectively?

3. What are the major powers of the Supreme Court?

4. What are the differences between the Democrats and the Republicans in terms of political
   ideology?

Chapter 5　Social Life

Think and Explore

Why is the U.S. educational system said highly decentralized?

Comment on the press freedom in the U.S.A.

What are American values and personality?

Ⅰ. The U.S. Education

Premise *n.*前提
Corollary *n.* 必然的
结果、推论
Touchstone *n.* 试金
石、检验标准

　　The current U.S. education system is built on two ideal premises: first, all must be guaranteed a basic education at the elementary and middle school levels — provided at public expense; and then, all must be guaranteed the opportunity and right to further education at a higher level. The above two premises, which reflect the notion of equality emphasized in American society, have also given rise to widespread controversy and, of course, their implementation has been closely monitored.

　　It is important to note at the outset that in the United States, the planning and implementation of educational services is in the hands of the individual states, rather than under the control of the federal government. In fact, this is a corollary to a series of historical reasons for distrust of government. In fact, the American people have longed for a strong, centralized government. But the truth gives the impression that "We don't want the government in Washington telling us what to teach our children." Local control of education is a touchstone of American democracy and also undoubtedly a feature of American society. Anyhow, the federal government, recognizing the importance of an educated civilian population for the benefit of the nation as a whole, has begun to intervene in many indirect ways in the educational process at different levels.

American egalitarians insist that all children must have equal access to a good education, regardless of racial and religious/cultural background, social class, and economic status. In American society, where the lines between rich and poor are distinct, there is a consensus that education must be publicly funded. Otherwise, the wealthy class will be given priority in education, which will eventually lead to a growing gap between the rich and the poor. Since "success in life" is closely related to education, all children must have equal access to education. In practice, however, this has proven to be a difficult goal to achieve.

The United States invests more in education than any other country in the world, so one would expect American education to be the best in the world, but the fact is that some countries do better than the United States, despite investing less money. This is a sad fact that is of deep concern to American educators. This is partly due to what was mentioned earlier — local control of education: education is invested locally, and economically distressed areas spend far less on education than economically affluent areas because of low tax revenues. Local funding accounts for 83% of the overall investment in education, while federal funding for education (indirectly through a variety of different funding programs) accounts for only 8.2%. In this way, students living in well taxed areas are fortunate to be in the best educational facilities. They enjoy the highest quality of education (including instruction by highly paid teachers). Conversely, students living in economically distressed areas have to deal with crumbling school buildings and teachers who are both poorly qualified and unenthusiastic about education.

Differences in local economic conditions lead to impacts on education and other consequences. In poorer areas, especially in the "inner city" areas of many cities, the social habits and high crime rates that accompany poverty have turned schools into potentially dangerous places. One of the major concerns now is whether parents can send their children to private schools with

Egalitarian *n.* 平等主义者
Consensus *n.* 一致意见
Priority *n.* 优先事项
Crumbling *a.* 崩裂的、衰败的
Tip33　美国教育与中国教育在哪些方面存在差异?

better educational conditions, but are concerned about whether they will be eligible for public funding. While the law states that parents are responsible for their children's education, the issue of public funding has not yet been resolved. An even greater concern is whether public schools will completely collapse if too many students and the corresponding public funds are transferred from public schools to private schools with the higher quality and safety.

Higher education in the United States, on the other hand, is based on the second premise mentioned earlier: all people should have access to a college or university. This has given rise to debate, with many believing that higher education should be available to those who do as well as possible in basic education, while others believe that it should be available to all who can benefit from it. Most publicly funded colleges and universities are trying to follow the second opinion by accepting as many applicants for admission as possible. Privately funded schools, on the other hand, follow the former view in particular, allowing admission only to those who excel in academic performance. Since the latter schools are also the most expensive, they often establish scholarship programs that are specifically designed to attract students who are truly gifted.

Just as American society values equality and individual autonomy and independence, American education emphasizes innovation and independent thinking. Ideally, American education accepts the idea that it is most important to teach students how to think, not what to think about. Teachers value their students' outspokenness and frankness, and encourage their spirit of argument and free inquiry. Whenever a teacher taught an alternative philosophical view of education that was well-known to students, chaos ensued in American school classrooms.

Throughout the history of the development of American education in the past century, American education has been shaped by various economic, cultural and political factors. Changes in society and a series of social reforms have influenced the changes in the American education system and eventually formed the present education system in the United States today. In the 1970s and 1980s, there was a strong call for "Back to Basics" in American education, and the public demanded that schools pay sufficient attention to the teaching of morality and ethics, as well as life and values. By the 1980s, however, there was a rapid and long-lasting leap forward in educational progress. During the post-World War II period, American education became more universal than ever.

The U.S. educational system is highly decentralized. Under the provisions of the Tenth Amendment to the U.S. Constitution, adopted in 1791, powers not delegated to the federal government but not prohibited to the states by the Constitution are vested in the states. The federal government therefore does not have the authority to determine the national education system, and education policy and curriculum development are determined by the states and local school districts. However, because of the commonalities in socioeconomic, political, and cultural aspects among the states, as well as the guiding role of the National Education Accrediting and Accrediting Agency, the education systems of the states vary, but are generally similar.

Education in the United States can be basically divided into three levels: primary education, secondary education, and higher education.

1. Primary and Secondary Education

In the U.S., you must be in school until you are 16-18 years old. Many states now require attendance until age 18. Some states only require attendance until age 14. Students can attend public schools, private schools or home schools. In most public and private schools, there are 3 levels of education: elementary, middle and high school.

Primary education in the United States includes one to two years of pre-school early childhood education, one year of kindergarten, and five to eight years of elementary education. Secondary education includes junior high school education starting in the seventh grade and senior high school education in the ninth to twelfth or tenth to twelfth grades. Most U.S. states implement free and compulsory public-school education from kindergarten through twelve years of high school. Funding for public elementary and secondary schools in

The structure of education in the United States

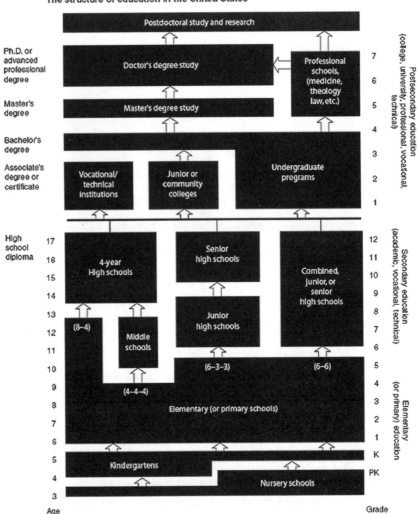

NOTE: Adult education programs, while not separately delineated above, may provide instruction at the elementary, secondary, or postsecondary education level. Chart reflects typical patterns of progression rather than all possible variations.
SOURCE: U.S. Department of Education, National Center for Education Statistics, Annual Reports Program.

SOURCE: U.S. Department of Education, National Center for Education Statistics

NOTE — Adult education programs, while not separately delineated above, may provide instruction at the elementary, secondary, or higher education level. Chart reflects typical patterns of progression rather than all possible variations.

the United States comes primarily from state and local governments. All U.S. states allow private elementary and secondary education, but they must be licensed by the state government, obtain a license to operate the school, and be subject to government oversight.

State and local governments in the United States manage elementary and secondary education in the following manner. Most states have boards of education that set public elementary and secondary education policies in accordance with relevant laws and regulations, which are implemented by state education directors and their subordinate professional educators and support staff. The responsibilities of state boards of education typically include allocating state education funds to local education authorities, enforcing or interpreting school-related laws, and advising local education administrations. Local school districts play a very important role in the specific management and operation of elementary and secondary education. The leadership of a local school district generally consists of five to seven members, some of whom are appointed by the local government and others are elected by the local residents. The board of education of the school district, which is composed of the leading members of each school district, charges the local education administration and its staff with the specific management of local public elementary and secondary education in accordance with state policies, etc.

2. Higher Education

Higher education in the United States has a history of 370 years, beginning with Harvard College, which was established in 1636. The operation and management system of higher education in the United States is relatively complex, in which the federal government, state governments and national organizations of higher education institutions play different roles as three key links.

Since the founding of the United States, the federal government has been actively supporting the development of higher education, but the federal government has never formulated any prescriptive documents on the operation and institutional aspects of higher education. Since World War II, the U.S. federal government has provided research grants and student financial aid to universities, which has had a profound impact on the U.S. higher education.

In addition, the federal government has supported higher education in terms of tax policy, such as providing tax deductions for funds raised by institutions of higher education and for educational expenses prepared by families for their children. Each state government in the U.S. has regulatory documents governing the planning, operation and institutions of public higher education in the state. However, in general, state governments only provide the legal framework for the operation of higher education institutions, while various national, regional or industry organizations formed by various types of colleges and universities play a very important role in the operation and institutional regulation of higher education institutions.

There is no uniform pattern for the allocation of higher education funds by the state governments in the United States, but most states determine the allocation scheme based on the actual situation. In other words, after the state government's annual budget for higher education is determined, the specific allocation plan is determined according to the annual enrollment of each public university in the state, the nature and needs of the school, and the condition of teaching facilities. In general, the amount of funding allocated to each state university does not vary significantly from year to year. The state government usually only sets some guidelines for the use of the funds.

There are many types of public and private colleges and universities throughout the United States that have a variety of teaching and learning focuses. Some are vocational training or technically oriented, others emphasize humanities education, and many are comprehensive colleges and universities that combine all of these academic areas.

In the United States, there are three main types of "colleges". The first refers to undergraduate educational institutions affiliated with universities (e.g. Harvard College and Yale College); the second is a liberal arts college that focuses only on undergraduate education; and the third is a community college. Among the above colleges, undergraduate colleges and liberal arts colleges are mainly four-year programs and graduates are awarded a Bachelor's degree, while community colleges are mainly (but not necessarily) two-year programs and students are eventually awarded an Associate's degree. Universities in the U.S. refer to research universities with both undergraduate and graduate schools. However, some U.S. "universities" retain the word "college" as their name for historical reasons (e. g. the College of William and Mary); other U.S. technical universities, which follow the European Polytechnic model, are called "Institutes" (e. g. Massachusetts Institute of Technology and California Institute of Technology).

3. Basic Statistics on Education in the United States

According to the statistics released by the U.S. Department of Education in 2004, the total number of students in the United States was 71.7 million in the fall of 2004, of which 55.1 million were elementary and secondary students and 16.6 million were college students. The total number of teachers in schools and colleges was 4.3 million, and the total number of other professional, administrative and logistical staff was 5 million. Thus, the total number of students and employees in the formal education sector is 81 million. This represents approximately 27% of the total U.S. population (nearly 300 million), or more than a quarter of the nation's population.

In the 2002-2003 school year, there were 14,465 public school districts in the United States. There were 71,270 public elementary schools, including 366 elementary schools with only one teacher. There were 28,151 public secondary schools. There were 26,569 private elementary schools and 11,846 private secondary schools.

In 2004, there were 4,236 general higher education institutions in the United States. Of these, 1,720 were public colleges and universities and 2,516 were private colleges and universities.

II. U.S. Mass Media

Although there is no special propaganda department in the United States, most of the mass media organizations are privately run. Their ownership and operation are not affiliated with any political party, so they seem to have a strong independence and operate according to the laws of the market, and seem to maintain a balance among several dimensions: politics, business, art, ideology and taste. But in reality, there is a clear government shadow behind the American mass media. The U.S. government uses a number of companies and institutions to produce a large number of "Hollywood" movies and dramas, publish a large number of newspapers, operate radio stations, online media and some mobile Apps, and export values to the world through a mature market mechanism. These media are well-produced, diverse, and beautifully packaged, and their values propaganda is concealed, not only achieving good results at home, but also attempting to establish U.S. "cultural hegemony" around the world. The U.S. mass media is the propaganda machine for U.S. values, which pervasively pushes the American way of life and values to all corners of the world, achieving a multi-win situation in politics, economy and culture.

Propaganda *n.* 宣传
Affiliate *vt.* 附属于
Inception *n.* 开端
License *vt.* 许可
Tip34 思考大众媒
体是如何输出文化价
值观,影响人们思维
认知的。

1. Newspapers and Magazines

At the inception of newspapers, the first official act restricting press publication was passed in the Massachusetts colony in 1662, requiring publications to be approved and licensed before they could be published. Since then, various newly founded newspapers have appeared. By the early 1830s, American publishers were no longer required to obtain government approval to start a newspaper, but the government enacted *The Libel Act*, which made newspapers legally responsible for their own statements, in order to prohibit them from speaking unfavorably about the government and to punish them with imprisonment if they were deemed guilty of seditious libel.

After the end of the American War of Independence, a bourgeois regime with a republican form of government was established. For more than half a century, parties have used the press as a tool to compete for power and profit, and newspapers have been largely dependent on political parties to promote their ideas and advocate for their interests. To a certain extent, this reflects the essence of the political party press — not so much a press as a propaganda and endorsement tool.

It is worth noting that although the U.S. press appears to be of mixed quality, ranging from major newspapers such as the *New York Times* and the *Wall Street Journal* to tabloids specializing in lacy news and sex magazines such as *Playboy*, they are united in the U.S. ideological strategy, and they all spare no effort in promoting U.S. values and maintaining U.S. "cultural hegemony". In addition, the U.S. newspaper industry seems to be highly commercialized, and its press freedom is based on the First Amendment of the Constitution, but the U.S. also attaches great importance to restraining press propaganda and consolidating ideology through laws, and a series of laws such as *The Defamation Act*, *The Espionage Punishment Act*, and *The Enemy Act* are the bottom line that the U.S. press cannot cross, especially in terms of national security, and the media are very careful.

2. Movies and TV

American movies are world-famous, and Hollywood movies are the benchmark of the world movie industry. 1896 was the beginning of American movies when Edison first showed films to the public in New York his Vitascope, which was very popular. After that, Edison set up a film patent company, which controlled almost all aspects of film production, distribution and projection, forming a monopoly on the film industry. In order to get rid of the monopoly and survive and develop, some film studios and producers went to Hollywood one after another to make movies, and in this way, Hollywood gradually became the center of American cinema and even world cinema.

In the 1920s, the rapid development of the American broadcasting industry exerted a great impact on Hollywood films. In 1929, the first Academy of Motion Picture Arts and Sciences Awards ceremony was held in Hollywood, which was later known as the Academy Awards. Eight major studios, such as Paramount and Warner Brothers, virtually controlled the entire film market. They were well-financed, with expensive studios, vast locations, and star-studded teams of big directors. In short, Hollywood films began to develop in the early 20th century, and after the perfection of the 1930s and 1940s, they reached their heyday in the 1960s and became the world's dominant film industry.

In order to regulate the development of the film industry, the Motion Picture Producers and Distributors of America (MPPDA), later the Motion Picture Association of America (MPAA) and the Motion Picture Association (MPA), was established and the Hays Code was promulgated. The Hays Code was an important piece of legislation in the history of the United States to restrict the censorship of film content, and had a profound impact on Hollywood films until the Classification and Ratings Administration (CARA) introduced the motion picture rating system in 1968. Nowadays, American movies are mainly divided into five levels: G (popular, anyone can watch, such as *Toy Story*), PG (counseling, some content may not be suitable for children, such as *The Hurt Locker*), PG-13 (special counseling, recommended for children after the age of 13, such as *Titanic*), R (restricted, recommended for children over the age of 17, such as *The Matrix*), and NC-17 (prohibited for ages 17 and under). In Hollywood movies, American mythology, American power, and American spirit can be found almost everywhere. Using the global influence of Hollywood films, American values are promoted around the world.

The American television industry was developed in the late 1920s. During World War II, the development of the American television industry came to a halt. After World War II, the U.S. television industry grew rapidly again, and television sets became popular in American homes, and watching television became the main form of leisure for Americans. In the political sense, the emergence of television changed the procedures and ways of American political campaigning, weakening the role of traditional parties, and the candidates' external charisma, expression ability and manners became important factors in determining the winner. In terms of content, news accounts for only 1/10 of U.S. television programs. The greatest function of U.S. television is entertainment, and the most influential is television drama. Television series are generally produced by the five major U.S. television networks. In the 1940s, "soap operas" emerged in the United States. In the 1960s, "soap operas" grew by leaps and bounds, with more than 10 airings per year, creating a boom in the United States. At the same time, the American drama has a wide range of subjects, cross-genres, interpretation means, strong audience participation distinctive characteristics, easy to be welcomed by the public. Because of this, the U.S. government continues to promote the American way of life, spirituality, and values through American dramas, and continues to influence people around the world.

3. Broadcasting

Broadcasting in the U.S. started early, with the first radio station established at the University of Wisconsin in 1919, which was mainly used to broadcast weather information and market news, and the 1930s and 1940s were the golden period for the development of the U.S. broadcasting industry. By 1943, the U.S. broadcasting industry was a triad of NBC, CBS and ABC.

The U.S. broadcasting was managed by the U.S. Networking and Communications Commission (FCC), a seven-member federal commission (changed to five after 1883), with commissioners nominated by the Senate and appointed by the President, who could not have a pecuniary interest in the entity being managed, and the commission director was appointed by the President among the commissioners. The FCC, as the highest executive authority in the broadcasting industry, is the "gatekeeper" of the broadcasting industry and has a significant impact on broadcasters. In 1934, the *U.S. Broadcasting Act* was enacted, providing clear regulations for the licensing and approval of broadcasting.

The most famous radio station in the U.S. for transmitting values abroad is the Voice of America (VOA). Founded in 1942, VOA was first affiliated with the U.S. War Information Agency and later placed under the U.S.

Information Agency, with government funding. At the beginning of its existence, VOA focused on World War II propaganda, but after the end of World War II, it began to shift its focus to anti-communist propaganda. In addition, there is Radio Free Asia in the United States. Radio Free Asia is nominally a private organization, but is actually part of the International Broadcasting Bureau (IBB), which is funded by the U.S. Congress.

4. The Internet and New Media

The Internet was born in the 1960s from the U.S. military network ARPANET, which was first used only for military purposes, but began to be civilized and commercialized in the 1980s. In 1995, the World Wide Web, a global information network, emerged, and the Internet was officially civilized and commercialized. In 1994, the first online newspaper appeared. Since then, the Internet began to challenge the traditional mass media and dominate the information system.

The Internet has broken through the time and space limitations of the traditional mass media, and its timeliness, convenience, secrecy, and wide coverage have brought about a revolution in the dissemination of values. In the United States, the most viewed website is Google; the most frequently

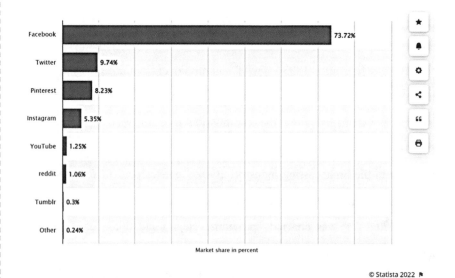

Leading Social Media Websites in the United States as of May 2022,

Based on Share of Visits

used social media is Facebook; Americans mainly get information from CNN, Fox News, *New York Times* and other media; young people mainly watch news through social media, such as Facebook, YouTube and Twitter.

The emergence of smartphones has driven the rapid development of mobile Internet in the United States. Now the mobile Internet in the United States has surpassed the PC access side, and the mobile network has become mainstream. Mobile Internet is becoming more and more popular, and most people spend more time on their phones than sitting in front of their computers.

Of course, within the U.S., although it claims to have a free press, regulation of the Internet is unrelenting, and it has some of the most comprehensive regulatory laws in the world. As early as 1977, the U.S. enacted *The Federal Computer Systems Protection Act*, pioneering the legal system of the network. For every step forward in the development of the Internet in the United States, the law will also follow a step forward. In 2012, the U.S. government introduced *The Internet Users' Privacy Bill of Rights* to make specific provisions for personal privacy and data security. In recent years, the United States has also set up various specialized agencies to regulate the network in all aspects. The U.S. also attaches great importance to international network security, and has invested a lot of human, material and financial resources in this area. Especially after the Snowden "Prism Gate" scandal, network security protection is more vigorous.

III. American Values

American national values, or American values, are the sum of the core values that the United States has held since its founding and the values that have been manifested in its national policies and institutions and in its national behavior. An examination of American values requires a deeper look at the history of American development.

The formation of American values dates back to the 1720s, a period that began with the Mayflower Convention, signed by a group of Puritans who arrived in America from Europe, and ended with the founding of the United States of America.

The Convention contains few words, but contains several important key words: God, citizenship, justice, equality, law, and so on. These key words outline the basic value principles of the founding of the United States, which are also the core values of the United States — liberalism and Protestant ethics, which also contain the spirit of contract that has been widely spread in the West since the Renaissance. It can be said that liberalism and the Protestant ethic constitute the DNA of American values.

After gaining national independence, the United States needed to express its philosophy and values clearly to the people in order to better unite the people in general and bring the country into a rapid and steady development. The Declaration of Independence calls out that "All men are created equal, and are endowed by their Creator with certain unalienable Rights, that among these are the Life, Liberty and the Pursuit of Happiness." This passage articulates the conceptual form of American values — liberalism. This value is highly compatible with the liberal spirit advocated by John Locke. Here we can see the desire of "Americans" for freedom, equality, and human rights and their vigilance against government power.

It is impossible to understand American society without an understanding of American Puritanism, which laid the foundations of American culture and influenced American society, its politics, and even its foreign policy in every way. In the beginning, it was under the fervent religious devotion to purify the world and build the "City of God" that the Puritans decided to colonize North America and gradually developed a national consciousness that the American nation was "God's chosen people". Later, this sense of being chosen was combined with expansionist ambitions, and the Puritans claimed to be following God's will to spread the Christian gospel and American democracy to every corner of the Western Hemisphere and the world. The "American Exceptionalism" and expansionist interventionist tendencies derived from Puritanism are deeply written into the DNA of American history.

Endow *vt.* 天生赋予
Unalienable *a.* 不可
转让的
Articulate *vt.* 表达
Compatible *a.* 兼容
的、协调的
Vigilance *n.* 谨慎
Fervent *a.* 热忱的
Gospel *n.* 信念、信
仰、福音

In the early stages of capitalist development, American Puritans used the rhetoric of "Manifest Destiny" and saw the primitive accumulation of bloody and violent capitalism as an act of religious piety. After the establishment of global hegemony, the United States further made Puritan "Manifest Destiny" the ideology of domestic and foreign affairs, and all peoples, nations and civilizations that differed from the Puritan tradition and American democracy were targets to be taught, domesticated and even eliminated. The dichotomy and extremism of the Puritan tradition has always profoundly influenced the United States.

Manifest Destiny 天赋
使命
Piety *n.* 虔诚
Domesticate *vt.* 驯化
Dichotomy *n.* 二分法
Tenfold *a./adv.* 十倍
的(地)
Foothold *n.* 立足之地
Barbarian *n.* 野蛮人
Exemplary *a.* 典范
的、模范的

1. Manifest Destiny and American Expansionism

The Puritans, with their strong religious beliefs, originally claimed to create a "City on a Hill" independent of the European continent. However, after its founding, the United States expanded more than tenfold in less than a century; by the 19th century, the United States continued to expand by millions of square miles in a massive "westward movement"; as the United States grew stronger, its territorial ambitions expanded from North America and the Western Hemisphere to the entire world. The U.S. was trying to gain a foothold in every part of the world.

Prior to the 19th century, the Puritans believed that territorial expansion was their religious vocation. This sense of mission first came from the British Virginia Company, which went to colonize North America, claiming it was not only for trade goals, but also to spread the holy Protestant gospel to barbarians on distant shores. After the American Revolution, the North American Puritans developed a strong sense of national pride, especially after the failure of the Glorious Revolution in England, and their belief in the exemplary nature of North America as the "Promised Land" became more pronounced. These Puritans became increasingly convinced that they were "God's chosen people" and therefore wanted to follow God's teachings to spread the Gospel of Christ and the Puritan order, and in their view, territorial expansion meant liberating the Indians from the old European colonizers and transforming their lives with superior Puritan ideas.

Providence *n.* 天意
Secularization *n.* 世俗
化
Millennium *n.* 千年
Missionary *n.* 传教士
Backwardness *n.* 落后

After the 19th century, the idea of providence was gradually bound to American freedom, and territorial expansion and institutional expansion became two sides of the same coin. On the one hand, the "Second Great Awakening" movement of the 1820s and 1830s contributed greatly to the secularization of Puritan theology in America. Ministers claimed that territorial expansion was a virtuous act, a sign of Puritan piety, and that accelerating territorial expansion would hasten the millennium. On the other hand, in the context of the decline of democracy in Europe, the sense of the American electorate was formally combined with pride in American-style democracy, and territorial expansion was seen by many politicians and missionaries as a way to spread both the Gospel of Christ and the "American freedom" and "American way of life".

Portrait of Columbia — the Spirit of Westward Expansion (Known as American Progress Painted by John Gast)

It was the Puritan idea of Manifest Destiny that provided the "moral support" for the logic of American expansion. On the one hand, Americans believed that there was a strict line between civilization and barbarism, between progress and backwardness, and they were willing to transform barbaric races and backward regions in accordance with the Mandate of Heaven, even if it meant bloody violence and militarism. Initially in North America, the Puritans slaughtered countless Indians in King Philip's War, claiming that killing these savage and inferior populations was the same as killing beasts and vermin, as was the mandate of Heaven. After the founding of the United States, this sense of distinction was repeated in American slavery, the Mexican-American War, and the U.S. colonial invasion of the Philippines, where white Puritans gave themselves the mission of "civilizing" the barbarian population, claiming that they would do whatever it took to transform what they saw as a backward and barbaric region with the so-called superior Puritan gospel and superior American democracy. On the other hand, the expansion of liberal capitalism was thus justified, and the United States was called upon by providence to seize raw materials, force commerce, and even colonize and invade, eventually gaining dominance over global commerce.

2. A Dichotomous Mindset

Puritanism had a profound impact in the United States, particularly in shaping the way Americans thought about self and other. Internally, Puritan philosophy ostensibly supported individualism, but in fact shaped an elite authoritarian model of rule. Initially, Puritan leaders boasted that they were agents of God's will and had insight into God's earthly wisdom to determine what was right and good in this world. The Puritan church required that all "regenerated" people in society be united, but the Puritans were only "free" to do what was right and good. This suggests that individual freedom was achieved by submitting to elite authority. This model of governance, in the name of individualism but in the name of elite dictatorship, has profoundly influenced the United States. The work ethic and consumerism of capitalism became the only right and good things to do under the control of the bourgeois elite, and individuals could only pursue a given "freedom" if they obeyed the work and consumer ethic. Externally, Puritanism has shaped a polarized

Barbaric *a.* 野蛮的
Mandate *n.* 授权(令)
Slaughter *vt.* 屠杀
Savage *a.* 野蛮的
Vermin *n.* 害虫
Mindset *n.* 思维
Ostensibly *adv.* 表面上
Authoritarian *a.* 独裁的
Regenerated *a.* 重生的、新生的
Dictatorship *n.* 独裁、专制
Polarized *a.* 极(端)化的

Outcast *n.* 被抛弃者
Assimilate *vt.* 同化
Mentality *n.* 心态、思想状况
Rogue *n.* 流氓
Per se（拉丁文）本身
Detriment *n.* 损害
Emerging countries 新兴国家
Tip35 清教思想如何影响美国人的国民性格和国家政策取向？

dichotomy that has made Americans accustomed to dividing enemies and friends, even to the point of actively seeking and creating enemies.

From "elect/outcast" to "civilization/savagery", the polarized thinking of dichotomy has always existed in the tradition of Puritan philosophy, and the history of the United States has been one of constantly defining and transforming "barbarism" and "backwardness", and constantly identifying and eliminating "enemies". The "enemies" of Puritan America were defined first as Great Britain at the beginning of the American Revolution, then as the Catholic dictatorship of Spain in the "Old World," then as fascism during World War II, as Soviet communism during the Cold War, and as the Islamic world in the post-Cold War era. Within the United States, races and religions other than white Puritans were either assimilated or rejected. Even in the contemporary world, where territorial expansion is an old dream, the United States still does not give up interfering in the internal affairs of other regions, countries and nations with the mentality of a "Chosen Elite Nation," who either they identify with American-style liberal democracy and become friends, or they are labeled as "rogue states" and become enemies of the United States. Under the mindset of "millennialism" and the expansionism derived from Manifest Destiny, white puritanism teaches that the United States should rule as a global elite and treat its "enemies/friends" with dichotomous thinking, and this underlying mindset is consistent in American internal and external politics.

As the only superpower in the world today, the United States was once the builder and maintainer of the existing world order, but now it has become the destroyer of the international order and the initiator of international crises. American values per se is fundamentally for the sake of its own freedom while ignoring the freedom of other countries. To a certain extent, American values have preserved the world order, but this order itself is more in the interest of the developed Western countries to the detriment of the emerging countries, especially the countries or regions with different ideologies.

IV. American Personality

1. Individuals Shape the Environment

Americans don't believe in "fate". They believe that each person should be in control of anything in his or her environment that could potentially affect him or her. Problems in someone's life are not so much the result of bad luck as they are the result of laziness and unwillingness to take responsibility for the pursuit of a better life.

2. Seeing "Change" as Inevitable and Positive

In the American mind, there is no doubt that "change" is a good thing, that it leads to development, improvement and progress. Many older, more traditional cultures believe that "change" means chaos and destruction; they value stability, continuity, tradition and historical heritage-none of which are very important in the American view.

3. Time and Time Management

For most Americans, time is extremely important. People want to be on time, be punctual, save time, use time, consume time, waste time, delay time, buy time, plan time, limit time, and even pass time. Americans place more value on getting things done on time than on developing relationships. Their lives seem to be controlled by that little piece of machinery they wear on their wrists that causes them to abruptly end discussions in order to make it to their next appointment on time.

4. Equality/Fairness

"Equality" is so cherished in America that it is considered to have a religious basis. Americans believe that all people are created equal and that everyone should have an equal opportunity to succeed. This idea of equality is difficult to understand for nine out of ten people in the world who believe that status and power are worth pursuing, even if they happen to be at the bottom of the social ladder.

5. Individualism/Independence

Americans consider themselves to be highly individualistic in their thoughts and actions. They do not want to be seen as representatives of any group that shares their interests. When they do join groups, they see themselves as special—more or less different from other members of the same group. In America, you will find people freely expressing all kinds of opinions at all times. Individualism brings privacy, and Americans value that. Americans often say, or even think, "I'd go crazy if I couldn't have a half hour a day to myself!"

6. Self-Reliance

Americans are only proud of what they have accomplished as individuals. They are not proud to be from a wealthy family, but proud to have climbed the ladder of success on their own, no matter what height they have reached. There are hundreds of compound words with the prefix "self" in the English dictionary, but it is difficult to find their counterparts in most other languages. It shows how much respect Americans have for those who achieve success through self-effort.

7. Competition

Americans believe that competition can bring out the best in any individual, in any system. This value is reflected in the free enterprise system of the American economic system and is applied in all areas of American life-health care, the arts, education, sports, etc.

8. The Future Comes First

Americans value the culture and progress that the future will surely bring. They devalue the past and largely ignore the present. Americans don't even pay much attention to immediate happiness because they believe that the future will bring greater happiness. Because Americans believe that humans — not fate — can and should take control of their environment, they are good at making plans for short-term projects.

9. Action/Work First

"Don't just stand there!" is the typical American advice to "do something". Although this phrase is usually used in emergency situations, in a sense, it speaks to the uplifting life of most Americans. It is a life in which action — any action — is always considered better than inaction. Americans routinely pack their day full of activities. Any rest and relaxation is time-limited and meant to "tune up" so that once they have rested, they can work harder. It is this "no nonsense" attitude to life that has created a large number of people known as "workaholics".

10. Unconventional

Compared to their Western European relatives, Americans are more unconventional and casual. For example, American bosses often ask their subordinates to call them by their first names, and are less used to being called "Mr. " or "Ms. ". The American dress code can best reflect this casualness, sometimes even casual to scary. For example, at a symphony concert in any major American city, you will see someone wearing blue jeans. The American way of greeting is also very casual. The more formal "How are you?" has largely been replaced by the informal "Hi. This is how people greet each other, whether it's a good friend or a boss."

11. Direct/Open/Honest

In many other countries, people use a more polite, sometimes highly polite, way of telling people bad news. Americans, on the other hand, prefer to be blunt. They tend to be blunt in their objections and tend to view all expressions that are not the most direct and honest as "dishonest" and "insincere". In the U.S., anyone who passes a message through a middleman is also seen as "controlling" and "untrustworthy.

Uplifting *a.* 鼓舞人心的
Inaction *n.* 不作为
Workaholics *n.* 工作狂
Dress code *n.* 着装规范
Symphony *n.* 交响乐
Blunt *a.* 直言的
Middleman *n.* 中间人
Untrustworthy *a.* 不值得信任的

12. Practicality/Efficiency

Americans have a reputation for being practical, pragmatic and efficient. When making any major decision, the priority is likely to be more practical. Will it make money? What's the bottom line? What do I get out of it? These are the questions Americans are likely to ask, they don't ask: Will it bring beauty and enjoyment? Will it be enjoyable? Will it increase knowledge? A preference for "practicality" has led Americans to favor certain professions. Management and economics are much more popular in the United States than philosophy and anthropology, and law and medicine are valued more than the arts.

V. American Friendship

The United States has a very different cultural background, and therefore the characteristics of their friendships are very different. Chinese people's collectivist values dictate that they believe in the interdependence of friends and place great importance on friendship and cooperation. Americans, on the other hand, are representatives of individualism and independent individuality, and friends are always in competition with each other. American friendship is strongly influenced by individualism and pragmatism. They are taught early to see themselves as independent individuals who are responsible for their own lives and future destinies. They do not like to be thought of as representatives of any of the same groups, but rather emphasize self-actualization and individual achievement, and focus on the "I" identity.

As a result, friendship is a very individualistic concept in American society. Americans rarely have deep and lasting friendships. They use the word friend very loosely and consider general acquaintances and close companions to be "friends". Their friendships are usually based on common interests, and may fade when the shared activities are over. Americans tend to make a friendly first impression. They often chat casually with strangers about their families, interests, hobbies and jobs. They may say enthusiastically with

Pragmatism *n.* 实用主义
Practicality *n.* 实用性
Anthropology *n.* 人类学
Tip36 总体而言,中美两国人民在哪些价值观念和性格方面存在较大差异?

178

a smile on their face: "Have fun, " "I'll see you later, " or "When are we going to get together?" But American friendliness is not always indicative of true friendship.

The same pragmatism that governs the American way of making friends emphasizes the importance of reality and the ultimate goal of achievement. In American society, in order to make friends, one must have the idea of "getting results". They see their friends as resources to help them achieve their goals, and their interactions with them as "means" to get things done. If things do not work out, they are likely to stop the current relationship and turn to others for the same purpose. This is why American friendships are relatively short-lived.

The Chinese are good at guessing the meaning implied between the lines, while Americans are taught from childhood to "express your meaning clearly". For example, a professor might say, "You did a great job" when praising his student. The American student is quite excited to hear this, and he is sure that the professor is quite pleased with him. The Chinese student, on the other hand, will think that the professor is just encouraging himself and that he may not be as good as the professor says he is.

Chinese people tend to use an indirect approach to inform others of unpleasant information, while Americans prefer to take a direct approach. They take a direct and open attitude in making negative comments and considering things. This can also lead to misunderstandings on both sides. For example, an American student wants to borrow a book from a Chinese friend. The Chinese friend politely refuses, "I left that book at my aunt's house". But the next day, the American student happens to see the book on the Chinese friend's bookshelf. He felt extremely dissatisfied and thought his friend was insincere. In fact, the Chinese student was not insincere, it was just a sign of their "smoothness". At the same time, Chinese people who value face should also know that the American "directness" is not intentionally not to give face. It is through mutual understanding that friendship can be further developed.

VI. Marriage and Family

It is generally believed that before the 1960s, the American family evolved from the extended family (a family consisting of at least three generations) to the nuclear family (a family consisting of a married couple and children under the age of 18). The extended family was the dominant family pattern from the early development of colonial North America to the industrialization of the 19th century. In the middle and late 19th century, with the rapid development of industrialization and urbanization and the acceleration of population mobility, the nuclear family emerged and gradually replaced the dominant position of the extended family.

After the 1960s, American values became more individualistic and sexually open, coupled with the rise of anti-traditional, anti-authoritarian, and anti-rational trends, and the rise of women's rights. With the rise of anti-traditional, anti-authority, anti-rational trends and the feminist movement, the American nuclear family was greatly impacted and the family model tended to diversify.

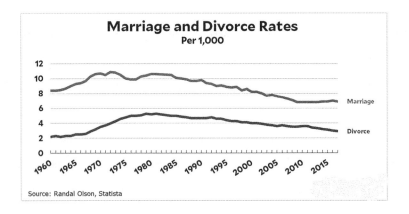

The proportion of two-parent families (i. e. nuclear families) has declined. The proportion of two-parent families, which used to be the mainstay of all family types, has declined sharply in recent decades. Specifically, the proportion of two-parent families is higher among Asian/

Pacific Islanders and Whites, and lowest among Hispanics and Blacks. 1) The number of single-parent families has increased. There has been a significant increase in the number of single-parent families, especially among women. Black single-parent households are the highest and Asian/Pacific Islander and White single-parent households are the lowest among all ethnic groups. 2) The number of single person households has increased. Since the 1960s, the number of single person households in the U.S. has been increasing, growing 3. 27 times over 40 years. Other family patterns include non-marital cohabitation and homosexual households.

Contemporary American marriages have also undergone significant changes, as evidenced by: 1) A decline in the number of people willing to marry, 2) A trend toward later marriage, 3) A gradual increase in the divorce rate. Among Americans, the divorce rate is lowest among Asians and highest among Blacks. 4) Inter-ethnic marriages. Since the 1960s, there has been a gradual increase in inter-ethnic marriages among Americans. 5) More people are living together outside of marriage. Until the 1960s, premarital sex was "studied and analyzed as transgressive behavior, and society confined sex to the marital relationship alone." However, with the popularity of the hippie concept of "free love" and "sexual liberation", non-marital cohabitation spread rapidly in the United States. 6) The rise of gay marriage. Before the 1960s, because homosexuality had long been considered a form of psychopathy in the United States, many homosexuals were afraid to reveal their identities. In the 1970s and 1980s, as the gay rights movement grew, the American public became more tolerant of homosexuals, and anti-discrimination policies and laws at the local, state, and federal levels included provisions against sexual orientation. It is estimated that there are as many as 1.2 million same-sex couples living together outside of marriage in the United States.

VII. Sports, Holidays and More

As in other countries, sports are an important part of national culture in the United States. American sports are very different compared to other regions. For example, compared to American soccer, baseball, basketball and hockey, soccer, which is a global phenomenon, is a relatively unknown sport in the U.S. However, as more and more teenagers play the world's most popular sport, soccer is considered to be the most promising sport in the U.S. In addition, the organization of sports in the United States is different from many other regions, as sports in the United States can still be a for-profit business, and many norms tend to be spectator-oriented, making a gap with the common international game, with some sports forming the norm of American dominance. In the United States, schools and universities play an important role in sports, even for professional careers, and many politicians are team captains in school, and the economic potential of sports competition revenue and sporting goods in the United States is very high. For a sports career is no less important than participating in international competitions, these sports stars earn even several times more than the national team players.

Sports are the most popular amateur activity in the United States and therefore have an extremely important social role. Many Americans either actively participate in sports activities or passively attend sporting events as spectators. In amateur sports there are amateur pastimes and amateur competitions. Among the amateur pastimes hiking, walking, boating, hunting and fishing are the most popular. The virtues embodied in sports such as teamwork, fairness, discipline and durability have a high reputation in American society. These virtues are especially evident in team sports such as baseball, basketball, football and volleyball, and therefore these sports are particularly popular among amateur sports. However, some single sports such as swimming, golf, tennis, bowling and track and field are also popular. The most influential amateur sports organization is the Amateur Athletic Association.

Americans also enjoy watching sporting events (either directly at the games or via television broadcasts): The most popular sports are baseball, basketball and American football. Rodeos are also popular in the Western states.

The U.S. government also sponsors sports. The U.S. government actively promotes and encourages national participation in sports.

1. Popular Sports

（1）Baseball

Baseball is so popular in the United States that many Americans played it as children, and it is therefore known as the "national sport" of the United States. Today's baseball originated as a children's game in the 19th century. Millions of spectators now go to professional baseball games each year, and many more watch the games on radio and television. Major League Baseball's season runs from April to October each year.

（2）Basketball

Basketball was invented in 1891 and quickly gained popularity. Today there are 250 million people playing basketball in the United States, and the United States has a monopoly on basketball power in the world and is also known as the Kingdom of Basketball.

There are 30 teams in the American professional basketball league, divided into two regions: East and West. The championship game between the two regions at the end of the tournament wins the title of the U.S. A. Basketball Champion.

（3）American Football

American soccer evolved from English soccer in the 19th century. It is one of the most popular sports in the United States, with thousands of players and millions of spectators each year. It is especially famous for its college team games. Today there are more than 600 college teams in the United States, with more than 35 million spectators each year.

American football, also known as rugby, is not commonly referred to as soccer. It is a tough, intense sport in which players wear protective masks and score points by playing with each other to win. The National Football League rulebook is 73 pages long, but the basic rules of the game are that the offensive team takes the oval-shaped ball and passes or runs with it, step by

step, to the bottom of the 100-foot (about 90 meters) field, eventually scoring a "touchdown" (touchdown) or field goal (field goal). touchdown or field goal to win.

American soccer's 56th Super Bowl championship game is coming up on February 13, and it will be the event of the day for millions of people in the United States and on their television sets. This year's game will be played between the Cincinnati Tigers (Bengals) and the Los Angeles Rams (Rams) at the Rams' home stadium in Southern California.

While the Super Bowl is a major sporting event with a rich history in the United States, it is also a cultural festival. Even those who are not interested in the game are likely to be invited to watch it with family or friends on this day. People gather at home, restaurants or sports bars to watch the game and eat snacks such as wings with hot sauce, mini sandwiches, and chips and nachos dipped in a variety of cheese and cream sauces and condiments.

(4) Ice Hockey

Hockey is the most popular sport in the United States and Canada after baseball, American soccer and basketball. The association for professional hockey teams is the National Hockey League. Like baseball, the league is divided into two divisions: East and West. The final 16 best teams compete in a knockout tournament to produce a champion, whose trophy is the Stanley Cup. Most teams come from the North due to natural conditions, but some teams come from the South and West.

2. American Holidays

The United States has 10 official public holidays a year on which the federal government is closed.

New Year's Day (January 1)

Martin Luther King Jr.'s Birthday (third Monday in January)

Presidents' Day (third Monday in February)

Memorial Day (last Monday in May)

Independence Day (July 4th)

Labor Day (first Monday in September)

Columbus Day (second Monday in October)

Veterans Day (November 11)

Thanksgiving Day (fourth Thursday of November)

Christmas Day (December 25th)

Thanksgiving Day and Independence Day (i.e. July 4) are two typical American holidays where friends and family usually gather to celebrate. On Thanksgiving, relatives will sit around for a big meal, with turkey being the traditional table highlight, while July 4 is dominated by fireworks, barbecues and baseball watching.

Thanksgiving Day, a national holiday in the United States and Canada located in North America, is closely associated with Christianity. The purpose is to give thanks to God for the past year's gifts and bountiful harvests. Thanksgiving is not celebrated at the same time in Canada and the U.S. In 1620, a passenger ship, the Mayflower, arrived from Plymouth to the Plymouth Colony in Massachusetts with a full load of Puritans (Calvinists). That winter, many people died of hunger and cold. With the help of the local aborigines, the new settlers learned to hunt, grow corn and pumpkins, and had a bountiful harvest the following year. On the day of the harvest, the newcomers from Europe took the traditional Thanksgiving form of the English

A Thanksgiving Day Dinner

Reformation and invited the native people to join them in giving thanks for God's blessings, which became the origin of American Thanksgiving. Like Canada, Thanksgiving in the United States had no fixed date in history and was decided by the states on an ad hoc basis until after independence, when it became a national holiday. From the time of the Founding Fathers until the time of Abraham Lincoln, each state had a different date for Thanksgiving, and in the early 19th century, most states in the United States customarily set Thanksgiving on the last Thursday of November.

The United States has always had a diverse culture, which means that holidays such as Passover, Eid, St. Patrick's Day and Labor Day are celebrated in a variety of ways in different regions. In New England, there are also regional holidays like Patriots' Day, which commemorates the first battles of the Revolutionary War. Many government offices and schools are closed on this day.

3. Tipping in the U.S.A.

Due to a loophole in the U.S. labor law, service industry employees such as waiters and bartenders are allowed by law to be paid less than the required minimum wage. This means they are paid only a few dollars per hour and therefore rely on tips from customers to make up the difference. In some U.S. cities, such as New York and San Francisco, there is a growing movement to eliminate tipping by paying employees in the service industry a living wage. "No tipping" restaurants always have signs stating that tipping is not necessary. The tip rate is 15% to 20% of the total bill. (Tipping tip: Shift the decimal places in the bill one place to the left and multiply the resulting amount by two to get 20 percent of the bill.)

However, it's not just bartenders and waiters who rely on tips to make a living. Often, tips are required for cab drivers, barbers, hotel cleaners, valet parkers, professional movers, food delivery drivers, and even tattoo artists! If someone in the U.S. provides you with a service that you don't want to do yourself, chances are you should spend a few extra bucks in return.

◎ Exercises

I. Choose the best answer from the four choices.

1. The U.S. educational system is highly _____. Under the provisions of the *Tenth Amendment to the U.S. Constitution*, powers not delegated to the federal government but not prohibited to the states by the Constitution are vested in the states.

   A. centralized
   B. decentralized
   C. dependent
   D. independent

2. In order to regulate the development of the _____ industry, the Motion Picture Producers and Distributors of America (MPPDA), later the Motion Picture Association of America (MPAA) and the Motion Picture Association (MPA), was established and the *Hays Code* was promulgated.

   A. radio
   B. film
   C. television
   D. Internet

3. The _____ , as the highest executive authority in the broadcasting industry, is the "gatekeeper" of the broadcasting industry and has a significant impact on broadcasters.

   A. CARA
   B. MPA
   C. IBB
   D. FCC

4. The _____ , with their strong religious beliefs, originally claimed to create a "City on a Hill" independent of the European continent.

   A. Catholics   B. Puritans

   C. Mormons   D. Baptists

5. In the 1970s and 1980s, as the _____ rights movement grew, the American public became more tolerant of homosexuals.

   A. gay   B. human

   C. civil   D. counter-culture

6. American football is more of a _____ type game in which the oblong shaped ball is thrown and passed as well as kicked.

   A. volleyball   B. basketball

   C. rugby   D. soccer

II. Decide whether the following statements are true (T) or false (F).

1. The federal government does not have the authority to determine the national education system, and education policy and curriculum development are determined by the states and local school districts. _____

2. Although there is no special propaganda department in the United States, most of the mass media organizations are not privately run. _____

3. It is impossible to understand American society without an understanding of American Puritanism. _____

4. Thanksgiving Day, a national holiday in the United States and Canada, has no connection with Christianity. _____

III. Give brief answers to the following questions.

1. How would you describe the differences in the understanding of friendship between Americans and Chinese?

2. What do you think is the most American of holidays for the American people? Why?

Appendix 1　Basic Information of the U.K.

Official Name	the United Kingdom of Great Britain and Northern Ireland	abbreviated as U.K.
National Symbols	National Flag: Union Jack	British National Emblem
National Anthem	God bless the King/Queen.	
Area	244,100 square kilometers	
Population	61.8 million (2008)	66.5 million (2018)
Capital Cities	London (pop. 8.6 million)	Other capitals: Edinburgh, Cardiff, Belfast
Major Cities	England: Birmingham, Manchester, Liverpool Scotland: Glasgow, Aberdeen	Wales: Swansea, Newport Northern Ireland: Londonderry
Climate	Temperate, Maritime	London temps. Range: 2℃-6℃ in January, 13℃-32℃ in July.
Religion	Church of England(Protestant), Roman Catholic	Minority religion: Judaism, Hinduism, Islam
Time Zone	Greenwich Mean Tim(GMT)	Summer Time: GMT+1 hr
Currency	Pound, Sterling	Symbol: £
Electricity	230 Volts, 50Hz	

Appendix 2   Basic Information of the U.S.A.

Official Name	the United States of America	abbreviated as U.S.A. or U.S.
National Symbols	National Flag: Stars and Stripes	National Emblem: Great Seal of the United States
National Anthem	The Star-Spangled Banner	
Area	9,629,091 square kilometers	land: 9,158,960 km^2; water: 470,131 km^2
Population	307.2 million (2009)	330.1 million (2019)
Capital Cities	Washington, District of Columbia (pop. 601,657)	
Major Cities	New York City, Los Angeles, Chicago, Seattle, Boston, Philadelphia, Houston, Miami, San Francisco	
Climate	Varied, mainly Temperate, Maritime	
Religion	Christian	Minority religion: Judaism, Islam, Hinduism, Buddhism
Time Zone	EST(GMT-5), CST(GMT-6), MST(GMT-7), PST(GMT-8) Alaska (GMT-9), Hawaii (GMT-10)	Summer Time: GMT+/-1 hr
Currency	dollar, cent	Symbol: $
Electricity	110-120 Volts, 60Hz	

Appendix 3　Chronology of Important Events of the U.K.

55 BC and 54 BC　Julius Caesar sends expeditions to England.

43　Roman Conquest begins under Claudius.

314　British bishops attend the Council of Arles, an evidence of an organized church in England.

406-410　Roman forces withdraw from Britain.

449　Jutes, Saxons and Angles land, and begin establishing the Anglo-Saxon kingdoms in England.

597　St. Augustine rebuilds Christianity in Britain and becomes the first Archbishop of Canterbury.

789-795　First Viking raids

899　Death of Alfred the Great, King of Wessex

1066　William, Duke of Normandy, invades and seizes the English throne.

1215　King John is forced to sign *Magna Carta* which set limits on royal power from abuse.

1265　The formation of Parliament

13th century　First Oxford and Cambridge colleges founded

1314　Robert Bruce defeats the English ensuring the survival of Scottish kingdom.

1337　Hundred Years War with France begins.

1348-1349　Black Death wipes out one third of England's population.

1455-1485　War of Roses

1477　First book printed in England by William Caxton.

1534　Henry VIII breaks with Rome, founding the Church of England.

1536-1542　Acts of Union join England and Wales legally.

1547-1553　Protestantism becomes the official religion of England under Edward VI.

1553-1558　Mary I (Bloody Mary) supports the return of Catholicism and burns Protestant heretics.

1558-1603　Reign of "Virgin Queen", Elizabeth I, and the Golden Age of the Tudors.

1588　English fleet defeats the Spanish Armada.

1590-1613　The plays of William Shakespeare are written.

1603　Union of Scotland and England when James VI of Scotland becomes James I of England.

1607　The first English colony established in Virginia

1642-1651　Civil War between King (Charles I) and Parliament

1649　Execution of Charles I

1652-1654　The First British-Holland War (Britain won)

1653-1658　Britain becomes a republic ruled by the Puritan Oliver Cromwell as Lord Protector. He abolishes the monarchy, the House of Lords, and the Anglican Church.

1660　Restoration under Charles II

1662　Founding of the Royal Society to promote Natural Knowledge

1663　John Milton completes *Paradise Lost*

1665　Great Plague

1665-1667　The Second British-Holland War (Britain lost)

1666　Great Fire of London

1672　The Third British-Holland War

1686　Issac Newton puts forward his laws of motion and the idea of universal gravitation.

1688　The so-called Glorious Revolution, a bloodless coup against the last Stuart monarch, James II

1689　*The Bill of Rights*

1756-1763　The Seven Years War between Britain and France

1760-1840　The first Industrial Revolution transforms Britain.

1775-1783　American Independence War under the reign of George III.

1776　Adam Smith's *The Wealth of Nations*

1793-1815　Anti-French Alliance (7 times)

1812-1815　The Second Britain-America War

1815　Battle of Waterloo and final defeat of Napoleon Bonaparte

1815-1914　Expansion of British Empire

1833　Abolition of Slavery in the British Empire

1836-1848　The Chartist Movement

1836-1870　Novels of Charles Dickens

1837-1901　The Big Ben and Reign of Queen Victoria

1840-1842　The First Opium War and *Nanking Treaty*

1851   The First World Expo in London

1857-1859   The First India Revolt

1856-1860   The Second Opium War and the *Peking Treaty*, the Summer Palace was burned.

1859   Charles Darwin published *On the Origin of Species by Mean of Natural Selection*.

1862   The world's first underground in London

1860s   The building of the Parliament House

1899-1902   The British-Boer War

1900   Siege of the International Legations

1901   *Final Protocol for the Settlement of the Disturbances of 1900*

1910-1936   The British Empire reaches its territorial zenith, claiming "the sun never set".

1914-1918   World War I

1918   Women receive the vote.

1919-1921   The Easter Rising and the Anglo-Irish War

1928   Alexander Fleming discovers penicillin.

1931   Australia, Canada and New Zealand became independent.

1939-1945   World War II

1946   Winston Churchill delivered the Iron Curtain speech.

1947   India and Pakistan win their independence.

1948   Britain's National Health Service (NHS) begins, offering free medical care to the public.
Independence of Burma

1949   Britain joined NATO.

1952-2022   Reign of Queen Elizabeth II

1950-1960s   Independence of Sudan, Malaya, Kuwait, Kenya, Zambia, etc.

1966   Egypt took back the Suez Canal.

1970s   North Sea oil and gas was found and exploited

1973   U.K. joined EEC.

1980s   Thatcherism

1982   Falklands War or Malvinas War between U.K. and Argentina

1984   *Joint Statement of the Chinese and British Governments on the Hong Kong Issue*

1997   China regains its sovereignty in Hong Kong

2012   London hosts the Summer Olympic Games

2016   The U.K. votes to leave E.U. in a referendum

2021   The U.K. exits from European Union

Appendix 4　Chronology of Important Events of the U.S.A.

1607　British London Company established the first colony in Jamestown, Virginia.

1620　Puritan pilgrims from England arrived in Plymouth, Massachusetts in "May Flowers"and they passed *The May Convention* in the boat.

1636　The first university, Harvard, in the United States was founded in Boston.

1752　Benjamin Franklin flew a kite in a storm, proving that lightning was a kind of electricity and invented lightning rods.

1774　The first Continental Congress was held in Philadelphia.

1775　Gun-shooting from Lexington

1776　Thomas Paine published the pamphlet Common Sense and the Continental Congress adopted the *Declaration of Independence* drafted by Jefferson.

1787　The Constitutional Convention was held in Philadelphia and a new Constitution was passed.

1789　The Federal Government was established and George Washington became the first President. The Supreme Court was founded.

1791　The Constitution was added ten amendments, *the Bill of Rights*.

1800　The Capital was moved to Washington D.C.

1803　The United States bought Louisiana from France, doubling its territory.

1807　A steam boat designed by Robert Fulton sailed from New York City to Albany.

1812-1814　the second war between the United States and Britain

1819　The United States gained Florida and Oregon from Spain.

1823　President Monroe in his annual address to the Congress introduced *Monroe Doctrine* against European intervention in American affairs.

1844　The first telegram was sent by Samuel Morse from Washington to Baltimore.

1846-1848　The Mexican American War broke and the New Spain was ceded to the

United States

1852 The novel *Uncle Tom's Cabin* written by Beecher Stow was published.

1853 Black Ship's Event

1854 *Japan US Goodwill Treaty*

1861-1865 The American Civil War

1862 *The Land Grant Act* was passed to establish state universities.

1863 The Emancipation Proclamation

1865 Abraham Lincoln was assassinated.

1867 America bought Alaska from Russia.

1869 The first transcontinental railway switched on.

1876 Bell invented telephone.

1879 Thomas Edison invented electric light.

1898 The United States declared war on the Spain.

1899 America put forward the Open Door policy.

Wright brothers succeeded in driving an aircraft with an engine.

1905 The Chinese Exclusion Law

1906 the worst earthquake in the history of U.S.A. in San Francisco

1909 Women Strike in Chicago (Women's Day)

1912 President Taft proposed the policy of Gold Dollar Diplomacy.

1917 The United States declared war against Germany and got involved in World War I.

The United States signed *Lansing-Shijing Agreement*, recognizing the privileges of Japan in Northeast China and Inner Mongolia in exchange of Japan's recognition of the Open Door policy.

1918 President Woodrow Wilson put forward *Fourteen Points* before the Paris Peace Conference.

1929 New York Stock Market plunged and the Great Depression began.

1933 Franklin Roosevelt became the President and took *New Deal* to coop with economic recession.

1941 The Japanese attacked Pearl Harbour and America declared war on Japan.

1944 Normandy Landing

Bretton Woods Conference established the dominant role of U.S. dollars.

1945 Declaration of Crimea and Yalta Agreement by the United States, Britain and the

Soviet Union

Potsdam Declaration by the United States, Britain and China.

Atomic Bombing on Japan

1946   the first computer

1947   Secretary of States Affairs, George Marshall, proposed a package of aids plan for the economic recovery of Europe, Marshall Plan.

1948   General Agreement on Tariffs and Trade (GATT, later WTO)

1949   North Atlantic Treaty Organization was founded in Washington Convention and the Cold War started.

1950   The Korean War broke.

1954   Senator Joseph McCarthy manipulated congress hearings to clean up the so-called communist influence across the country.

Start of *Civil Rights Movement*

1959   Alaska and Hawaii became states of the U.S.A. in sequence.

1961-1973   The U.S. - Vietnam War

1962   Cuba Missile Crisis

1963   A grand demonstration calling for equal rights for the black was held and Martin Luther King delivered a speech *I Have a Dream*.

President Kennedy was shot dead.

1969   The spacecraft *Apollo* II landed on the moon and human set foot on it.

Demonstration against Vietnam War

1972   President Nixon visited Beijing and Shanghai Communique was announced.

1973-1975   Oil Crisis and Oil-Dollar Regime

1974   Watergate Scandal and the setup of GPS

1979   China and U.S.A. established formal relationship.

1979-1980   Tehran Hostage Crisis and Reaganism

1986   The American Space Shuttle *Challenger* exploded. Reagan's Irangate

1990   Desert Shield Operation was taken to protect Kuwait from Iraq's invasion.

1990s   Internet Boom and Bubble

1994   *North America Free Trade Area Agreement* came into force.

1995   World Trade Organization (WTO)

1999   NATO attacked the Federal Republic of Yugoslavia.

China and U.S.A. completed the bilateral negotiation over China's entry to WTO.

2001   Terrorist Attack on World Trade Center, September 11th Event

2001-2021   Afghanistan (Anti-terrorism) War

2007   Financial Crisis

2018   Sino-America Trade War

References

1. B. W. E. Alford. *Britain in the World Economy Since 1880*[M]. New York：Routledge，1996.

2. Cochrane，Willard W. *The Development of American Agriculture：A Historical Analysis*[M]. University of Minnesota Press，1993.

3. Datesman，Maryanne，et al. *American Ways：An Introduction to American Culture*[M]. Pearson，2014.

4. Evans，K. M. *The American Economy*[M]. Information Plus，2007.

5. Gay，Jackie. *This Is America*[M]. 天津：天津人民出版社，2017.

6. Mauk，D. & Oakland，J. *American Civilization：An Introduction*（7th ed.）[M]. Routledge，2017.

7. Norbury，Paul. *Culture Smart*! *Britain*[M]. Kuperard Publishing，2015.

8. 陈奕平. 当代美国人家庭与婚姻模式的演变及其影响[J]. 世界民族，2006(2)：60-70.

9. 韩毅. 美国经济史 17—19 世纪[M]. 北京：社会科学文献出版社，2011.

10. 胡国成等. 21 世纪的美国经济发展战略[M]. 北京：中国城市出版社，2002.

11. 来安方. 英美文化与国家概况[M]. 上海：复旦大学出版社，2020.

12. 李巍. 制度变迁与美国国际经济政策[M]. 上海：上海人民出版社，2010.

13. 史宝辉，訾缨. 英语国家概况[M]. 北京：北京大学出版社，2010.

14. 王恩铭. 英语国家概况[M]. 上海：上海外语教育出版社，2013.

15. 王湘云. 英语国家文化[M].北京：首都经济贸易大学出版社，2020.

16. 谢福之. 英语国家概况[M].北京：外语教学与研究出版社，2013.

17. 张少华. 汉密尔顿"工商立国"与杰斐逊"农业立国"之争[J]. 历史研究，1994(6)：126-141.

18. 朱永涛，王立礼. 英语国家社会与文化入门[M]. 北京：高等教育出版社，2013.

19. https：//www.britannica.com/.

20. https：//www.bbc.com/news/business.

21. https：//www.statista.com/topics/6632/leisure-activities-in-the-united-kingdom-uk/.